THE PSYCHOLOGY OF MUSIC

THE
PSYCHOLOGY OF MUSIC

H. P. KRISHNA RAO

GYAN

Published by

Gyan Publishing House
5, Ansari Road
Daryaganj, New Delhi-110002
Phone: 011-47034999, 9811692060
E-mail: books@gyanbooks.com

Distribution Network
gyanbooks.com
India, USA, Canada, UK, Australia, France

ISBN : 978-81-212-2870-1 (HB)
First Published, 1916

2nd Impression 2021

Printed at: Gyan Press, Delhi.

The
Psychology of Music
Author: H. P. Krishna Rao

THE PSYCHOLOGY OF MUSIC

PREFACE

The lecture on "The Psychology of Music" was written for the All-India Music Conference held at Baroda on the 20th March, 1916, under the patronage of H. H. the Gaekwar. When explained in the Conference, it evoked in musical circles not a small amount of interest on account of the novel method adopted in treating the subject of music. A strong desire was expressed in high quarters to arrange for the delivery of the lecture again in Baroda, Bombay, and Poona; to publish it in the leading journals of India, and to translate it into the principal vernaculars of the country so that it may be available to the general public. In order to meet these pressing demands, it was found necessary to revise the lecture and publish it in book form.

Dr Westharp, Music Doctor of London, rightly complains that the musicians of the present day have, especially in the West, been more and more abandoning the true sphere of music. The inner beauty of the musical sounds is ignored and their emotional value destroyed. Attempt is therefore made in this book to show that every musical note has its own characteristic feeling to express, and that music is but the language of emotions. If the author has not succeeded in convincing the readers of the truth of his statements, the fault is with himself; for the subject is so difficult that only the language of Burke and the logic of Bain can do full justice to it.

Let the kind reader feel the subject sympathetically; let him examine it on the touchstone of his heart, he is sure to find it interesting as well as instructive.

Laksmipuram,
Mysore,
1-9-1916.

H. P. KRISHNA RAO.

CONTENTS

THE PSYCHOLOGY OF MUSIC

CHAPTER I.

The Definition and Nature of Music

THE word *language* comes from Latin *lingua*=the tongue. It now denotes any means of expressing or communicating thoughts and feelings. In the usual sense, *language* means a system of conventional signs; that is, *words* or *gestures* having fixed meanings.

It is common to divide language into two classes: the spoken language and the written language. This classification is very rudimentary, inasmuch as the written language is merely a visible representation of the spoken one. It also excludes several gestures which are as significant as the spoken language. The correct division of language should therefore be into three classes:—(1) the sound-language, (2) the sign-language and (3) the word-language. A word has only a conventional meaning, while a sound has a natural meaning. Sounds are distinguished by *pitch* and words by letters.

Man comes out of the mother's womb with the sound-language. He cries for milk, he cries for sleep and he cries for comfort. This cry is essentially musical. It gives the mother great delight to hear his voice, which stirs her heart more than any music of the world. As months elapse, the baby can see, and as it grows, it expresses its feelings and thoughts by means of the sign-language. The word-language comes in an advanced age. But when man grows old, words become shaky and make room for gestures, and at last—alas!—the sound-language, the moan (the slur), or the jerk (the staccato) leads him onward to the grave. Music! The blind may not acquire the sign-language and the dumb may not know the word-language. Your shades never forsake man in pain or pleasure, in birth or death. Wonderful are your powers!

The function of all these three forms is to communicate one's thoughts and feelings to others. The sound language originates from instinct, and develops into the art of music as cultivated by different nations. It consists of inarticulate sounds, which are termed notes in music, and which proceed chiefly through the vocal chords. The sign-language originates from instinct and reason, and consists of signs and gestures in which the limbs of the body—the hands, the face, the lips, the tongue, the brows and the cheeks—come into play. The ancient *Natyasastra* of the Hindus, the art of dancing among the Europeans, and the methods of lip-reading and signalling come under this class. The word-language is based chiefly upon reason, and consists of spoken words uttered by means of the palate, the tongue, the teeth, the lips and the nose. Grammar, philology and literature deal with the word-language.

In the expression of thoughts and feelings, all these three forms, though distinct, co-operate with one another. When Antony addressed the Romans thus,

> Friends, Romans, countrymen, lend me your ears ;
> I come to bury Cæsar, not to praise him.
> The evil that men do lives after them ;
> The good is oft interred with their bones,

he certainly called to his aid the gestures of his hand, and spoke in a varying pitch of voice. A person engaged in a quarrel uses his fists and utters hot words in a changing tone. A songster uses articulate words along with certain gestures.

The sign-language is the most intelligible form, but less perfect. The word-language is the most perfect, but artificial. The sound-language, though less intelligible, is very effective. The sign and the sound-languages are common to man and the lower animals. Man understands the signs of animals and likes their sweet notes. Likewise, the animals are capable of knowing his signs, and feel the power of his music. Hence there is no cause for wonder when it is said—

> " Sisur Vetti Pasur Vetti Vetti Ganarasam Phani "
> The child knows, the brute knows,
> And the cobra knows the sweets of music.

The spoken language, being artificial, is confined to man only, and it can express thoughts directly and feelings indirectly. The sign-language expresses thoughts and feelings directly, but music can express only feelings and emotions directly and thoughts indirectly. Music is, therefore, primarily a language of feelings and emotions, common to man, the brute and inanimate nature. Corresponding to the word-language, it has, as a science, its own alphabet, its own words, grammar and literature ; and as an art, its own pleasing elements of beauty.

It is a well-known fact that a musical note pleases the ear while a noise displeases it. Let us see why it is so. The difference between a musical sound and a noise consists in the fact that the former arises from *regular* vibrations of the air. The only cause that is most essential to give rise to agreeableness is regularity. Regularity is the order of nature. The planets move round the sun in regularity. They also move round their own axes in regularity. The years roll by in regularity. The seasons, the tides, the day and the night, come and go in regularity. Man's birth and death take place in regularity. Youth and old age, and their millions of organic changes, exhibit themselves in regularity, and, in fact, the plant life and the animal life are bound up in their growth and development by strict rules of regularity, obedience to which means pleasure, and disobedience pain. What a grand power is regularity!

Again, embryology teaches us that in the mother's womb the nervous system develops much earlier than the heart, which begins to beat in the third or in the fourth month. Consider the effect of its beating. It is again a work of regularity. The heart propels blood throughout the body, and by means of arterial pulsation the whole nervous system is drilled into a discipline of regularity. The soft and impressionable nervous substance is so much furrowed with regular impressions, that every impulse coming from outside in regularity is received agreeably and every irregular impact causes an inconvenient displacement of the molecules of the nerves, and gives rise to a feeling of disagreeableness. Hence a musical sound originating from regular vibrations pleases the ear, while a noise displeases it.

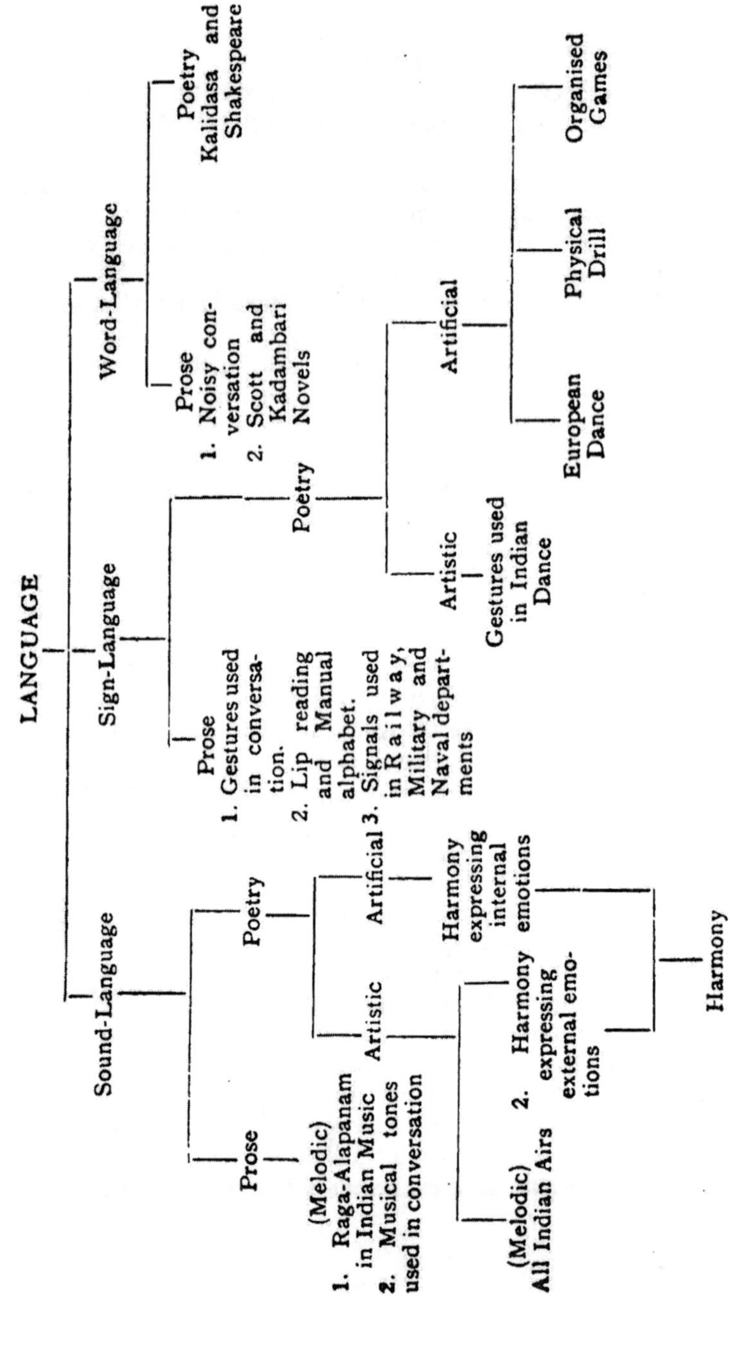
LANGUAGE
Sound-Language
Sign-Language
Word-Language
Prose
(Melodic)
1. Raga-Alapanam in Indian Music
2. Musical tones used in conversation
Poetry
Artistic
Artificial
(Melodic) All Indian Airs
2. Harmony expressing external emotions
Harmony expressing internal emotions
Harmony
Prose
1. Gestures used in conversation.
2. Lip reading and Manual alphabet.
3. Signals used in Railway, Military and Naval departments
Poetry
Artistic
Gestures used in Indian Dance
Artificial
European Dance
Physical Drill
Organised Games
Prose
1. Noisy conversation
2. Scott and Kadambari Novels
Poetry
Kalidasa and Shakespeare

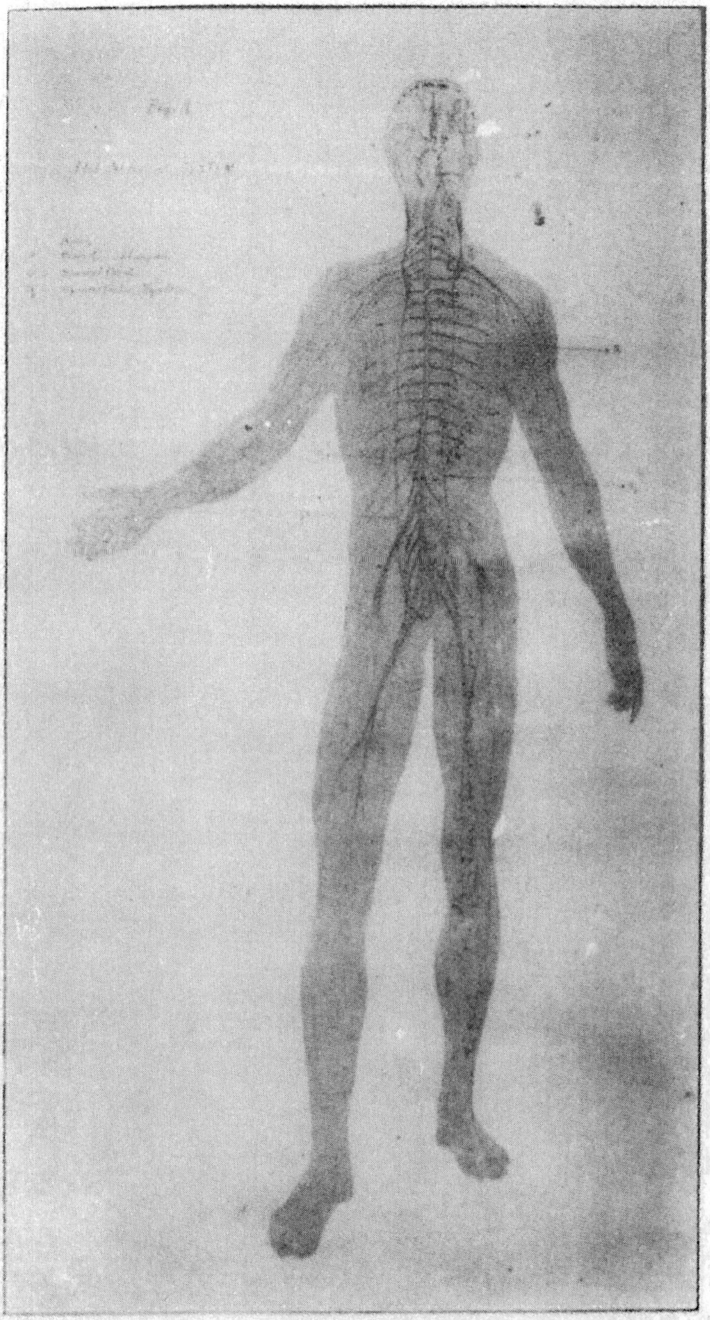

CHAPTER II

The Nervous System and Its Function

(Adapted from Prof. Huxley)

THE human body consists, as that of every other animal, chiefly of bones, muscles and nerves. The bones support it; the muscles move it; and the nerves, like telephone wires, guide it. The nervous apparatus with which we are more concerned consists of two sets of nerves and nerve centres which are connected together. These are the cerebro-spinal system and the sympathetic system. The former consists of the cerebro-spinal axis, composed of the brain and the spinal cord, and the cranial and spinal nerves with which they are connected with this axis. The latter comprises the chain of the sympathetic ganglia, the nerves of which they give off and the various cords by which they are connected with one another and with the cerebro-spinal nerves. The spinal nerve consists of two branches, the sensory and the motor. The sensory nerve carries an impression to the cerebral organ, and the motor nerve carries away that impression from the central organ to effect specific changes in certain portions of 'e body. Sometimes the cerebral organ enters into a state of activity without our being able to trace that activity to any direct influence of changes in sensory nerves. The activity seems to take its origin in the cerebral organ, and the movements to which it gives rise are called *voluntary*. Putting these cases on one side, it may be stated that a movement of the body, or any part of it, is to be regarded as the effect of a stimulus applied to the ends of sensory nerves, which set up a molecular change in their substance, which change is propagated from molecule to molecule along the fibres to the central organ with which they are connected.

The molecular activity of the sensory nerve sets up changes of a like order in the fibres and cells of the central organ; from these the disturbance is transmitted along the motor nerves, which pass from the central organ to certain muscles. A similar disturbance is also set up in the substance of the muscular fibres, which contract and relax in various ways. Such a series of molecular changes is called a *reflex action.* The eye-lids wink at a flash of light; the whole body starts at a loud noise; a sweet sound creates instantaneous pleasure. A bad smell causes a grimace. These are due to reflex actions. Reflex actions proper to the spinal chord are natural, and are involved in the structure of the chord and the properties of its constituents.

By the help of the brain we may acquire an infinity of artificial reflex actions, that is to say, an action may require all our attention and all our volition for its first or second or third performance, but by frequent repetition it becomes, in a manner, part of our organisation, and is performed without volition or even consciousness. "As every one knows," says Prof. Huxley, "it takes a soldier a long time to learn his drill—for instance, to put himself into the attitude of '*Attention*,' but after a time the sound of the word gives rise to the act, whether the soldier be thinking or not." There is a story which is credible enough, though it may not be true, of a practical joker, who, seeing a discharged veteran carrying home his dinner, suddenly called out "*attention*". Whereupon, the man instantly brought his hands down, and lost his mutton and potatoes in the gutter. The drill had been thorough, and its effects had become embodied in the main nervous structure.

The possibility of all education is based upon the existence of the power which the nervous system possesses, of organising conscious actions into more or less unconscious, or reflex, operations. Also, it may be laid down as a rule which is called the *Law of Association* that if any two mental states be called up together, the frequent production of one of them will suffice to call up the other, and that whether we desire or not.

In the early stages of the education of a child such words as *stone*, *tree*, or *Rama* are repeated to the young mind. Their spelling and meaning are explained several times. These impressions take firm root in the nervous structure of the brain, and if after some time the words are heard, their meaning and spelling come up to the mind of themselves. Many habits in life are formed likewise, and they are likley to be repeated just as before, even without the action of the will. Habit is, for this reason, termed "second nature." The brain is, therefore, a store house of impressions which are conducted to it by the sensory organ.

It is now necessary to grasp the difference between a simple sensation and a complex one. A sensation given rise to by the irritation of a single nerve fibre is a simple sensation, but most sensations are compounds of different simultaneous sensations, or present sensations with past sensations, or with those feelings of relation which form the basis of judgments. When we hear a sound we are compelled to think of the agent emitting the sound, its physical and mental state, not only at the time of hearing the sound but both before and after.

Another important fact to be borne in mind in connection with music is this:—whether a nerve is stimulated by a natural cause or an artificial one, the effect produced as a result of the stimulus is the same. The interference of the will hardly controls the physical change, and the struggle between the will and the reflex action is so doubtful in result that it is the latter that generally gets the upper hand. We have experience of persons who, at the sight of even mere representations on the stage, are moved to tears without being able to control themselves. Men of weak will and nerve should not stay in areas of epidemic, since the fear itself may set up a reflex action and lead to the actual suffering of the disease. The nervous system, and especially its sensory part, is therefore just like the keyboard of the piano, which, at the mere touch of any agent, the finger or the stick, gives rise to the same sounds and feelings. It is not a rare occurrence that at still hours the mewing of cats is often mistaken for the cry of little babies and rouses tender feelings. The sound oooo (moan) proceeds generally from a person who is suffering from some acute pain. It reminds of the previous experience and causes pain to the hearer even when the sound proceeds from some other source. Or the deep sound ooooo, caused by the passing of a strong current of wind through the window, sometimes reminds us of the hooting of an owl.* The owl reminds of its abode in a deserted building, which conveys an idea of ruin, desolation, and ultimately of some unknown calamity. In the development of the reflex action and association the following stages are interesting to note—

o-o-o-o-o-o-o-o-o-o-o-o reminds of the owl (1)
(the sound of wind)
o-o-o-o-o-o-o-o-o-o ... „ its abode (2)
o-o-o-o-o-o-o-o-o ... „ ruins (3)
o-o-o-o-o-o-o-o-o ... „ cause of ruin (4)
o-o-o-o-o-o-o-o-o-o ... „ unknown fear (5)
o-o-o-o-o-o-o-o-o ... leads to muscular changes result-
ing from fear if the act of destruction is referred to self; or pity if referred to the once occupants of the ruins. As the reflex action firmly establishes itself in the constitution, all the intervening stages disappear, and the sound of o-o-o-o brings on the ultimate stage of thrill or throb, which fact is so well taken advantage of by makers of modern motor cars, who have transformed the sweet note of the horn, sounded by way of caution to the passengers, to diabolical yells, as appear to have been borrowed directly from Dante's Inferno. When sounds of varying curvature in pitch are introduced into music, associations which these sounds convey in real life are called up, and suitable feelings are expressed by means of the reflex action, giving vent to sighs, sobs, throes, laughs or tears. The will may know the real origin of sound full well, but it may or may not be able to control the muscle. Hence association and reflex action play the most important part in music, in converting sensations of sound into those of feelings and emotions, and every sound in music carries with it a train of associated feelings, which affect the heart most by their sweet indefiniteness of expression.

* It is generally held among the Hindus that the owl is an inauspicious bird and any dwelling-house on which it alights is sure to go to ruins. This belief is supported by the fact that the bird lives only in uninhabitable caves or buildings which once flourished but have now become desolated owing to some misfortune.

CHAPTER III.

The Will-Power and the Nerve-Power

IT is very interesting to note that the intensity of emotion depends upon the strength of the reflex action facilitated by the yielding nature of the nerve-substance. A man of nervous temperament, that is, a man of nervous constitution, very readily yields to external impressions. His heart feels instantaneously. The mind knows it, and can control the effects of feeling through the will-power.

Emotion, like heat or electricity, is a form of energy, and when it enters the body, its active power depends upon the quality of the nerve-substance over which it spreads. If the substance is a good conductor, if we may borrow the term, the human frame is thrilled with emotion, and it requires a strong will-power to control it. Love, joy, pity, kindness, anger, and hatred,—all these emotions find a ready response in a person of soft nerve, and he is very easily carried away by the stimulus. A musical sound similarly moves a person of this kind, and gives him immense pleasure. Where nerve-power preponderates, sudden outbursts of joy or sorrow are emitted, and they are easily apt to be cooled down as soon as the current passes away. Men of such constitution can never harbour any germs of mischief long in their mind. Such persons turn out, if criminals (which God forbid), very useful approvers, and a very good musical treat provided. for a gang would point out the best person for an approver, sooner than the liquor or the whip.

Where emotion and will are equipoised the results are satisfactory. But where the nervous substance is a non-conductor of emotion, it absorbs emotion slowly and retains it for a long time. The reflex action is so slow and mild that it does not move the muscle to any vigorous work. When a strong will is guided with a good motive, the result is only a mechanical display of good feelings. But if it is guided with an evil design, like that of Iago, it can contain and develop its schemes of viciousness and consummate them with great deliberateness to a successful though dangerous end.

Let us now describe the battle that takes place in the human frame between the will-power and the reflex action, or the nerve power. Let O be the origin and OX represent the line of increase of nerve power, and OY, perpendicular to OX, of the will-power. From the centre O, at the distance OX, draw a circle. Consider now the quadrant XOY. Millions of radii run from the centre O to every point in the segment, and each of these lines represents, as the result of the will-power and the nerve-power, the emotions of individuals of various constitutions and temperaments. When the two powers (will and nerve) are equal, the line *OZ* bisects the right angle XOY, and represents a well-balanced mind. The more the line *OZ* moves towards OY the will power becomes stronger and the nerve power weaker. Softer feelings then disappear. A man of stern disposition grows more and more hard-hearted, and passes through the stages of bad, wicked, cruel and murderous. He is not moved by music. As the line *OZ* moves more and more towards OX the will-power decreases and the nerve-power increases. A man becomes more and more yielding to emotion. He becomes kinder and kinder. He is soft-hearted. He is carried away with music. The angle XO*Z* is therefore the musical angle, and angle *Z*OY the unmusical angle. Capacity to appreciate music depends upon the position one occupies in the quadrant, and man's qualities, good or bad, depend upon his position in the figure.

When Shylock demanded a pound of flesh from near the heart of Antonio, was there any pity in him? He knew that pain would be caused by cutting up a man alive. There was the association of pain, but the reflex action was too feeble to withstand the power of the will. His was a nervous constitution at 85° on which the sweet strains of music could not have made any impression, or, in other words, he was thoroughly unmusical. The figure on *OZ*, inclined at 45° on the bisector of XOY, represents Justice. She is neither merciful nor cruel. Since her face is directed towards OX she is disposed towards mercy. "Give the benefit of doubt to the accused," is one of her

FIG. B.

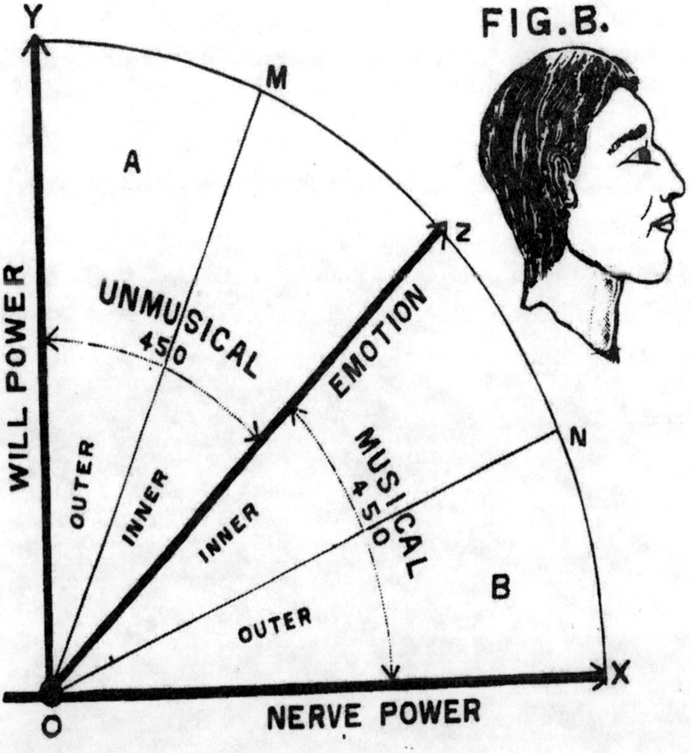

Y
M
A
Z
UNMUSICAL
45 0
EMOTION
WILL POWER
OUTER
INNER
INNER
MUSICAL
45 0
N
B
OUTER
X
O
NERVE POWER

maxims. Again, under the instigation of King John, Hubert determines, with a strong will-power, inclined at 90° along with OY, to put out, with the help of executioners' the eyes of young Arthur, and says to them—

Hub. Heat me those irons hot, and look thou stand
Within the arras; when I strike my foot
Upon the bosom of the ground, rush forth,
And bind the boy you shall find with me
Fast to the chair; be heedful; hence, and watch.

. . . .
. . . .

Arthur. No, indeed, is't not, and I would to heaven
I were your son, so you would love me, Hubert.

Hub. (aside). If I talk to him, with his innocent prate
He will awake my mercy which lies dead;
Therefore I will be sudden and dispatch.

This shows that Hubert is naturally merciful, but by a strong will, he has subdued his better parts. At this stage he has fallen down from 90° to 75°. After being shown the warrant of death,

Arthur. Have you the heart? When your head did but ache
I knit my handkerchief about your brows,
The best I had, a princess wrought it me,
And I did never ask it you again
And with my hand at midnight held your head,
And like the watchful minutes to the hour
Still and anon cheered up the heavy time,
Saying, 'what lack you?' and 'where lies your grief?'
Or 'what good love may I perform for you?'

Moved by such appealing words, Hubert came down gradually to 45°, and says,

Hub. Well, see to live, I will not touch thine eye
For all the treasure that thine uncle owes.

How reasonable was Hubert! and how kind! It is men of such constitution that are influenced by music. The more a person approaches the line OX, the more merciful he will be and more soft-hearted; but a reflex action through OX would result in the absence of control through the will-power, in heart-break, to which only nervous people are subject; or in suicide, as in the case of Romeo and Juliet.

CHAPTER IV

Music and Education

SEVERAL controversial problems, which prove of great interest to the theosophist, the medicinist, the fatalist, the politician and the educationist may be solved with the aid of diagram B.

The influence of heredity on man, or the methods of educating him when young or old, may be studied in its light. We will, however, deal only with education in relation to music.

Man's action is the result of the exercise of the will power and the nerve power, or, in other words, of the mind and the body. If the action is to be fruitful, a sound mind in a sound body is most essential; and these two could be acquired by sound education. But, the word 'Education' is derived from Latin *e*=out, and *duco*=to lead, and is understood at present as denoting "to lead out one's innate good qualities," or to improve upon his natural aptitude. The definition cannot hold good in all cases, for every man is not born with good qualities, some are born good and some wicked. The method of education must, therefore, vary with individuals. It must be positive as well as negative. If the angles Y*OZ* and XO*Z* are bisected by the straight lines OM and ON, the angle MON represents the angle into which every youth must be led by means of education. Persons, as explained before, are born with different degrees of will-power and nerve-power. They differ in nature as metals. While iron should be softened by heat, gold should be hardened by alloyage. In the case of persons stationed at A, the nature of education must be of a negative kind, calculated to bring down their wicked tendencies, and in the case of those born at B, its aim ought to be of a positive nature. In either case a youth must, by judicious means, be *led out* of the outer angles YOM and XON, and put in the angle MON as near O*Z* as possible. In the case of those born in the angle MON, their innate powers may be developed on the principles of education now in vogue.

The sound-language, *i.e.*, music with which the baby enters the world, is to be the medium of instruction in the early part of life, as advocated by Frœbel. The nervous system will thereby be regulated and it will contribute to muscular development. The sign-language, consisting of different signs, ought then follow in its two-fold divisions of dancing as an art and games and athletics as a science, thus making physical education a very important factor. The word language which aims at training the intellect is the last means of instruction that should be utilised. It is, therefore, of the greatest value that music should be the first subject of instruction in the educational curriculum of every country, and gymnastics the next. These two branches develop a sound body, in which a sound mind finds a very comfortable home.

But the nature of music introduced, and the words set to it, are to be such as to further the objects of education. While on the one hand the emotions of a person at A are to be softened by appropriate songs, those of the other at B will have to be hardened, the object being mainly to bring about an equilibrium of the nerve and the will powers, or equalise the physical and mental education tending to create a sound mind and a sound body.

An unmusical person near A is, as a member of society, a mechanical being. If he is well-educated, he may reach OZ. He does everything as a duty. He is devoid of sympathy, much less of pity. He is hard-hearted. He is deep in thought, reserved and strategic. Musical training in his case tends to soften his feelings, but he loves the art and enjoys it no better than he does prose or poetry. Judicious musical instruction, begun at a proper age, does much to train the nerve and sow the seeds of sympathy into the very substance of his constitution.

An unmusical person without education is worse than a brute. He is, like Shylock, a danger to society. Of him Shakespeare says—

> The man that hath no music in himself,
> Nor is not moved by the concord of sweet music,
> Is fit for treasons, stratagems and spoils ;
> Let no such man be trusted.

It may be enquired why the poet did not use the following form of expression:—

> The man that hath music in himself,
> And moves others by concord of sweet music,
> Is not fit for treasons, stratagems and spoils;
> Let only such men be trusted.

The reason is that the negative involves a caution to the musician and a consolation to the layman. A strong-willed person may, by studying the art well, become a very clever musician. But having no predisposition to soft nervous impulses, he may, like the Emperor Nero of Rome, who was playing on the violin when the city was on fire, be a traitor and tyrant; while a sympathetic person, being always engaged in the busy pursuits of life, may not be able to appreciate the beauty of music, though his nerves are tender, pliable and impressionable and he may still be a very kind hearted person. It is, therefore, an unmusical and uneducated man that is really mischievous.

A musical person with a sound general education is an ornament to society. Stationed on the line *OZ*, he can oscillate like a pendulum to OX or OY, according to circumstances. He it is that knows the right and the wrong. He feels for the sick and helps the poor. While the unmusical person dresses a wound mechanically like the surgeon, the musical person weeps for the wound as if he himself has sustained it. The motive for doing good proceeds in him instinctively, while that of the unmusical person is based on reason. The musical person is a friend in need, a dear partner, a loving parent and a loyal subject.

A musical person without education is generally a man without principles. Vice and virtue appear alike to him, though his nervous education disables him from taking part in any inartistic sin. He is propelled by instinct. Reason is at a discount. Being near to OX, he can hardly rise up to *OZ*. But he is godfearing and obliging. He is also sociable and amorous.

But every rule has an exception, and the general statements made above do not apply to certain individuals. Capacity to learn music or appreciate the art depends upon several physical conditions. A musical sound has to pass through the tympanum, the middle-ear, the sensory nerve, the brain, before it can extend its influences over the body through the motor nerves. These different physical agents, concerned in the production of a musical effect, must be healthy. A defect in any of these stages may vitiate the whole of the statements made above. We have among us eminent professors of music who cannot put two strings in unison owing to bad tympanum. We have also musical experts who, owing to nerve weakness, cannot keep the 2-4 time either when they themselves sing or when others do so. A perfect musician satisfies all these conditions. Such a man is a genius.

Though the advantages of musical education combined with the physical are patent to every one, the system of education all over the world, as constituted at present, creates a great gulf between these two branches of education and the mental education. The latter receives full recognition and support at the hands of the colleges. Will-power is cultivated and the development of nerve-power is neglected to a deplorable degree. The rising youth grows, therefore, precocious in intelligence, becomes more sensitive, attains his majority while young, and dies a comparatively premature death with a shattered nervous constitution. As long as college buildings taper to the skies in the direction of OY, and leave their gymnastic halls on the ground-level in the direction of OX; As long as we find within academical walls anæmic professors and asthmatic lecturers, who soon after the evening bell retire to their rooms and exercise no healthy influence upon the students on the play-ground, as in the class-room, the pretensions of higher education are hollow and its advantages superficial. When will our universities rise to the level ? And when shall we have compulsory music and physical examinations, which will befit both the student and the teacher for their several duties and responsibilities in the world ?

Religion, it must be added, forms, in combination with music, another means of improving the character of man. The seeds of religious education are sown in him at a very early age, while he is yet an infant. He is impressed with the grandeur of nature—the sun, the moon, the stars, the wide expanse of the ocean, and the high mountains. All these give birth to a sublime feeling in him; and as he advances in years his spirit develops in the direction of enquiry. Till his very last moments, he is engrossed in the admiration of natural phenomena as mighty manifestations of the Unknown, when compared with the imbecility of his own poor self. Evey man is thus stirred up with religious emotion, and music, if added to its expression, unites most harmoniously. Religion and music are in themselves, capable of softening the beastly qualities of man, and a combination of the two is sure to bring about wonderful results.

But religion is the only agent which succeeds where music fails, and which can really tame unmusical persons. General education has no effect upon a class of unmusical people whose innate beastly tendencies do not yield to its cold decrees. It is only the religious feeling that can make them social and sympathetic. Their motive for doing good proceeds from fear of punishment, while in the case of others it proceeds from a sense duty or love. In any case, religious education improves a man's character and it does so much better if united with music.

It is not true that music is born of religion. Music expresses religious emotion just as it does any other. Only the relationship between music and religion is so time-honoured that the two appear as being inseparable. Religious worship was accompanied with music, even when man was a savage; but sexual love, which of late has appropriated music, received the aid of music only in an advanced stage of society.

Sexual love had not attained in primeval days that degree of refinement which the etiquette of modern civilisation has called into existence. Primitive man was nude, and only a few leaves of trees served, if at all, as his clothing. Love was based upon instinct. As time went on, barks of trees, cotton goods, silks and muslin came into use; social rules were framed, and they regulated the conduct of the sexes towards each other. Taste in speech, gait and dress attained a high degree of perfection, so much so that each of these adjuncts of life came to be looked upon as accomplishments (with voluminous treatises expounding their virtues). Under these circumstances courting became an art and sexual love a mystery. Its pains and pleasures became themes of high poetic effusion, and music soon lent its helping hand to its achievements. Music fanned the flame of love better than it did religion, though its embers were short-lived, while religion and music formed a healthy combination, producing eternal bliss. For purposes of education, it is necessary to combine religion and music, as in the case of Bhajans which are in vogue in India to-day, as the best forms of such combination and train the young in principles of morality and good conduct. A perfect system of education must, therefore, be based upon music, gymnastics, religion and general education.

A country in which there is no musical education is far behind in the scale of civilization. Its people are selfish and inhospitable, and wanting in that trait of character which makes them love and be loved by others. Music is sympathy, and it is desirable that the prince as well as the peasant should be musical. That country in which the ruler is musical will be happy, contented and prosperous, for he rules not by force of his sceptre but by his heart, which finds a ready response in every subject. Instances may be given from history to prove the fact that every musical sovereign has been a great benefactor to his country and his people. In fact, the state is a body politic, the governing power represents the brain, and the subjects so many nerve centres. The sovereign of the State can exercise a powerful influence upon them, and mutual sympathy depends upon the way in which they are educated. They resonate to the vibrations transmitted to them from the brain, and a reflex action, for better or for worse, is established in them.

Just as the State can govern the subject by sound musical education, it is possible for every parent to shape the social policy of his children. A musical child is a sympathetic child, and its tender qualities grow with age. The nature of the education given to it, must be such as to control its tendencies within proper bounds by the teaching of high principles of morality. The nature of the society the youth keeps should be carefully watched, and in the case of highly musical children the age of marriage should also be regulated. A musical child guided under proper surroundings and in the right path, is sure to grow obedient, intelligent and sympathetic. A musical soul is like pure gold, and its shape depends upon what its owner gives to it.

CHAPTER V.

Psychology of Musical Notes

PSYCHOLOGY is the science of the mind. It teaches us how to examine our own mind, and what changes it undergoes from time to time under certain influences. Just as a doctor observes the changes in the physical condition of his patient under the influence of a particular drug, the psychologist observes the changes which the mind presents under different conditions. "The process of observing our own mental processes is called introspection." There is another method of studying the mind. We may observe the bodily changes in other people, and then infer the changes of their mind. This method is called interpretation. We shall, by means of introspection and interpretation, examine the changes which the mind undergoes under the influence of musical notes.

The psychological study of music, both in the East and the West, is in a neglected condition. Many ancient Indian writers have written upon the subject, but their inferences do not stand the test of scientific enquiry. Western scholars have, by slow degrees, developed a system of music in which art and nature are so antagonistic that the prospect of their being able to succeed in the psychological study of music is very remote. Such an eminent scientist as Herman von Helmholtz says—

"Music has hitherto withdrawn itself from scientific treatment more than any other art. Poetry, painting and sculpture borrow at least the material for their delineations from the world of experience. They portray nature and man. Not only can their material be critically investigated in respect to its correctness and truth to nature, but scientific art-criticism, however much enthusiasts may have disputed its right to do so, has actually succeeded in making some progress in investigating the causes of that æsthetic pleasure which it is the intention of these arts to excite. In music, on the other hand, it seems at first sight as if those were still in the right who reject all 'anatomisation of pleasurable sensations'. This art, borrowing no part of its material from the experience of our senses, not attempting to describe and only exceptionally to imitate the outer world, necessarily withdraws from scientific considerations, the chief points of attack which other arts present, and seems to be as incomprehensible and wonderful as it is certainly powerful in its effects."

This is true of Western music. We feel sorry for it and we invite the earnest reader to follow us in our observations.

We shall now sing the musical notes in the octave, one by one, and examine the mental as well as physical changes that they give rise to. It is known that every state of feeling and emotion has its own characteristic form of speech, expressive of its shades and delicacy. The face and the features are also most susceptible to movement under feeling, the face being by pre-eminence the index of the mind. Several feelings have bodily accompaniments—joy, sorrow, fear and anger have their own distinct manifestations, called their natural language, the same in all ages and in all peoples. Even the thought or recollection of joy or anger brings on the same expression of countenance, the same gestures as the real passion. It is here that psychology and physiology co-operate with each other, and invoke the aid of painting and sculpture for the demonstration of their principles.

There are seven musical notes S, R, G, M, P, D, & N. The eighth note is the same as the first and is called its octave. The range of the notes from S to S is also called an octave. These notes are either Prakrita (natural) or Vikrita (accidental). The simplest way of representing the 13 notes of the octave is thus:—

S R_1 R_2 G_1 G_2 M_1 M_2 P D_1 D_2 N_1 N_2 S

Only three octaves are recognized in Indian music (see First Steps in Hindu Music in English Notation written by the Author). The notes of Mandra (lower) octave are indicated by a dot below; those of the Madhya (Middle) octave have no dots; those of the Tara (higher) octave are denoted by a dot above thus:—

Mandra Notes:—$\underset{\cdot}{S}\ \underset{\cdot}{R}\ \underset{\cdot}{G}\ \underset{\cdot}{M}\ \underset{\cdot}{S}\ \underset{\cdot}{D}\ \underset{\cdot}{N}$

Madhya Notes:—S R G M P D N

Tara Notes:—$\dot{S}\ \dot{R}\ \dot{G}\ \dot{M}\ \dot{P}\ \dot{D}\ \dot{N}\ \dot{S}$

S denotes one unit of time; Sa two units; Saa three units and so on, a unit being equal to a crotchet in duration.

$\overline{S}$, the line above S reduces its time by one half. $\overline{S\,a\,a\,a}$ is equal to only Sa. Two lines above a note reduce its time to one-fourth thus, $\overline{\overline{S}}$ a$=\frac{1}{4}+\frac{1}{4}$ (S a). A dot added to a note lengthens it by one half. These few symbols are enough for the purposes of this book.

We begin with the Sa of the Madhya Sthayi. Generally, the note is as high as the usual speaking voice of the singer. The muscular effort required in the production of the note is only very little, since the vocal chords have been accustomed to it from infancy. The face becomes bright, calm and composed. The eyes are almost closed. The sight is void of purpose and concentrated inwards. The cheek muscles are quite relaxed. There is no wrinkle on the brow. All other limbs of the body are quite at ease. In fact, the face expresses that state of mind which yogies assume while meditating upon the Brahman or the Supreme Being, or which new-born babies present when quiet.

Western musicians are in the habit of singing or playing music without the drone. They strike any two or three notes together, and call them major or minor seconds, thirds, and so on. Excepting the rough idea as concords and discords, these chords convey no artistic meaning. To judge the inner meaning of a musical note and its effect upon the mind, a sweet drone, as given by the Tambora, must always accompany the notes. For the purposes of judging the effect, only vocal music should be used, since instrumental music is a translation of real music, and cannot express the spirit of the original.

Weeping, laughing and quarrelling would lose all their emotional value if the voice employed in the act was of the pitch of the speaking voice. The higher it is raised the greater the effect of the laughter or quarrel, and in judging the degree of emotion a comparison with the speaking voice is always implied. In music there ought to be a permanent pitch, to compare the emotion of other notes. So the necessity of drone in music. Western music appears to be always off the rails, or it is like a curve in mathematics without its co-ordinates.

We now proceed to R, the Komanrishab of the Hindustani music, and Sudba Ri of the Carnatic School. This note slightly upsets the mind, but the feeling given rise to is one of disturbance of a very mild kind, with a tendency to drop down into Sa. The eyes are partially opened, the state of feeling is similar to that slight disturbance which a person in sound sleep feels when waked up, and soon after falls into slumber without exercising the will.

Then comes Tivra R_2 or Chatusruti Rishaba. The pitch has now sufficiently increased, and has grown strong enough to wake up from deep sleep the mind which has now been aroused to full consciousness. It calls for the

With less mirth, Fig. 1 represents R_1.
Fig. 2 ,, G_1

exercise of the will, which becomes attentive. The eyes are now wide open. There is no disagreeableness in R_2, as in R, for the will is at work, but when G_1 is reached a sensation of uneasiness is clearly felt. In this note a plaintive mood is expressed. In G_2 a soft but inquisitive tone as to the cause of the disturbance may be detected. M_1 then succeeds as a note, in which the disturbance is referred to self. Self-appreciation, conceit, haughtiness and self-assertion are expressed. The next note, M_2, is a very miserable note indeed. In it, impotency, self-abasement and misery are visible, and pain is expressed. The soul longs for immediate relief and finds it in the higher P. This is the way in which feeling passes from a state of tranquillity to pain. The same stages of feeling are traversed by the mind in its progress from P to the higher S as those experienced in its passage from S to P. The difference is, that in the former case the plane is one of a higher consciousness. The calmness felt at S (lower) is a feeling without any previous history. But the feeling felt at P is a calm after a storm, or pleasure after pain. Every note in the higher tetrachord is thus a reflection of the one in the lower. It is the force of the inner meaning of the musical notes that makes Indian music superior to all other systems in the world.

Before corroborating the truth of the above statements according to recognised principles of psychology, two illustrations, which roughly describe the state of feelings expressed by the several notes, may be given. Suppose A is travelling by train on a pleasure-trip, say from Bombay to the hills. His saloon is furnished most tastefully; his bed is one of silk and fur, and he falls into a happy reverie of slumber as he is whirled along. This state of the mind is expressed by S. On his way to the destination, a friend steps in and pulls his covering. A feels the pull, wakes up, feels drowsy, and falls again into sleep. This drowsy feeling is expressed by R_1. The friend is an obstinate one. He will not leave A alone. He gives A a stronger pull. A wakes up and wishes him good morning. A is now conscious of his surroundings. This state of mind is expressed by R_2. Uneasiness now follows, owing to the loss of comfort and sleep, which state of feeling is expressed by G_1. The reason for the disturbance is enquired into afterwards in G_2, and is found to be due to the presence of an intruder. Selfishness and self-dignity are expressed in M_1 and when the friend does not budge, pain, due to inconvenience, is expressed in M_2, but at the next station the friend fortunately alights and gives A great relief, which is expressed by P.

It is useful to give another illustration—of a sanyasi and his piece of cloth. The story is futile and not credible, but a high moral is commonly drawn from it. His life resembled that of Buddha, the prince, who having enjoyed the sweets of life left his wife and child in the palace and retired alone into the forest, as we all know. This poor sanyasi in question was, while only a baby of two or three months, in a state of happiness which was pure, simple and innocent, expressible by the note S. The faculty of hearing and seeing developed after some time. It could receive vague impressions, but not direct its attention to objects. It was the state of R_1. Many more months rolled on; the infant could recognise sounds and forms. It reached the stage of R_2. But having grown into a boy of seven or eight years, he had to spend a life of uneasiness, corresponding to the state of G_1, of having to abide by discipline. As a youth of eighteen, with a sound body and a sound mind, he saw the world in sympathy with his inquiring nature, as in G_2. As a man of dignity, expressed by M, he had his own ideas, his own principles and an opinion of his own. But some time after he found no attraction in his surroundings; he grew despondent, as in M_2, renounced the world, retired into a forest and became a sanyasi. Having thus secured a peaceful state of mind, as expressed by P, he sat in penance. Alas! he was not to be left undisturbed in the state of spiritual ease. A piece of cloth, very necessary for the order of a sanyasi, was being eaten away by a rat. Disturbance again cropped up. The uneasy state of D_1 appeared. So he thought of a remedy at D_2. He reared a cat to devour the rat, and was in the D_2 state, but the cat required a cow for milk, the cow a boy; the boy grew up to be a man and married. The burden of supporting the family again fell upon the Sanyasi; and in this way he found himself even in the higher plain of consciousness as miserable in N_1 as before. Seriously contemplating his miserable condition in N_2, he quitted the world altogether, and became one with Brahman in the higher S.

This story is related only to show the phases of the mind produced by the musical notes :

S and P are tranquil notes.

R_1 and D_1 indicate disturbance.

R_2 and D_2 are perceptions.

G_1 and N_1 indicate disagreeableness.

G_2 and N_2 indicate enquiry.

M_1 denotes optimism or egoism.

M_2 denotes degradation.

The lower tetrachord refers to the sensual plain of consciousness, and the higher to the intellectual.

Higher and lower octaves are only reflections of this principal octave.

CHAPTER VI.

Musical Notes

(Continued)

EVERY sensation of sound gives rise to a state of consciousness which consists of three factors:—Cognition (knowing), Feeling (pleasure or pain), and Attention. When the stimulus is of an agreeable nature the quality of feeling is one of pleasure. The Indian singer selects a note, for starting music, of the pitch of the speaking voice to which he is accustomed, and in the production of which he feels no sort of pain. To keep this pitch constant the drone is used, and all other notes are judged with reference to it. In singing Sa there is cognition and a feeling of pleasure, which is of a massive nature. The attentive element is directed inwards, and there arises a condition of deep sleep or self-absorption, on a lower plane, of the kind which rishies attain in meditating upon the Supreme Being. The mass of incoming currents through all other senses is kept out, and, in the words of an eminent psychologist, "The sensation of sound is flowing, unperceived like a tiny rill, through a broad flowery mead." Other currents may show their faces at the door, but they are turned back. Consciousness may, therefore, be said, so far as the outer world is concerned, to be at the zero point. It is also said to be plunged in a condition of "deep sleep." Now let O be the point of this state of consciousness, Fig. C. It is a fundamental psychological principle that increase in the stimulus leads to increase in sensation. Let OX represent the line of increase of stimulus, and OY its perpendicular, the line of increase of consciousness; *OZ* will then represent the resultant line of the feelings aroused, in proportion to the strength of the stimulus. When R_1 is sung a sensation of disturbance in relation to the first condition of deep sleep is felt; "for there is no series of absolutely independent sensations, but every sensation is determined by its relation to the one experienced immediately before it, or at the same time." If the very same note R_1 had been heard at first, it would have, to a great extent, conveyed a sensation of deep sleep of emotion. Since S has already been chosen as the convenient starting point, R_1 conveys an idea of disturbance. It is a sensation. The feeling is one of very slight pain. Attention is directed outwards. But the stimulus, being very weak, the attention tends to recede, and with it the state of consciousness.

"The next impression which a sense organ transmits by rising in pitch, produces a cerebral reaction in which the awakened vestige of the last impression plays a part. Another sort of feeling and a grade of higher consciousness are the consequences. Ideas about the object mingle with the awareness of its mere sensible presence. This higher consciousness is called Perception" as in R_2. From perception the next step is G_1, which is a note of disagreeableness, and hence some slight pain is felt.

The "Physiology of pain," says William James, "is an enigma. One might suppose separate sensory fibres with their own end-organs to carry painful impressions to a specific pain centre. Or one might suppose such a specific centre to be reached by currents of overflow from other sensory centres, when the violence of their inner excitement should have reached a pitch; or one might suppose a certain extreme degree of inner excitement to produce the feeling of pain in all cases." We cannot accept this view as correct. The sensation of pain is due not to the existence of separate pain-nerve centres, which is contrary to the law of the economy of nature or to any overflow of feeling. Pain is due to the inconvenient vibration of the molecules of the nerve fibre, its intensity being proportional to the degree of inconvenience. In G_2 there is enquiring; in M_1 there is egoism. When M_2 is reached intense pain is felt.

"In the stream of consciousness these states of tranquillity, disturbance, perception, uneasiness, enquiry, egoism and pain represent resting places. These are occupied by sensorial imaginations of some sort. The peculiarity is that they can be held up before the mind for an indefinite time.

"These places of flight are filled with thoughts of relations that for the most part obtain between the matters contemplated in the periods of comparative rest." From this point of M_2 the stream of consciousness falls into a calm lake, as it were, P, which is full of retrospective associations, and then overflows into a higher plane of consciousness in the same way as from S to P. The emotions ascribed to the several musical notes are thus true not only according to experience, but also according to scientific methods of study.

Young babies, rishis and yogis generally express Sa in their countenance. Lazy and morose persons exhibit R_1 ; intelligent persons indicate R_2 ; unhappy persons, G_1 ; lawyers and judges, G_2 ; rulers and princes, M_1 ; beggars, M_2 ; and happy people, P. Higher notes are reflections of these notes, and they can be expressed by all faces under different conditions. Laughter, coquetry and rage are expressible by ragas with the help of the word-language; but it is possible to say what note can express a particular face while it is not influenced by any emotion. The thought of nobility or beggary creates a feeling of that quality in the mind, and produces a corresponding facial expression. By the constant exercise of these feelings, assumed or natural, the muscles of the face get accustomed to the particular expression automatically, and become hardened in that position. The very sight of the face can therefore indicate the nature, rank and position of an individual in society. The haggard face of the miser, or the majestic face of the ruler, is the effect of the hardening of the muscles brought about by a series of reflex actions set up by the mind. It must be within the experience of many among us that the actors of a dramatic troupe, though born of low parents, develop, by constant representation of characters, appropriate powers of speech and physical expression. The actor who plays generally the part of the "King" shows the air of that personage even outside the stage; the baffoon is of that character even in the street, and he who plays the part of the heroine is often taunted and tormented everywhere for his womanish behaviour.

All musical notes in the octave thus represent different kinds of facial expressions, and conversely every calm countenance may be referred to a musical note.

Perception.

CHAPTER VII.

Notation and Music

FOR the purpose of instructing classes, or for preserving language for the benefit of all ages, it has been found necessary to invent a set of visible symbols, called *Notation*, which represents the elements of the language. Every kind of language must have its own notation. The notation used in the word-language is called its alphabet; the notation for the sign-language has not yet been formulated in the West or the East, as the sphere of the language extends over a very wide area. The elements of the language, i.e., signs used for the expression of thoughts and feelings, are divisible into "natural" and "artificial." Dumb persons and elocutionists use natural signs more than ordinary persons, whose gestures are generally ignored on account of their accompanying the clear expression of the word-language. However, the eyes, the brows, the cheeks, and so many other muscles of the face, take part in the expression of the sign language, that it would be a gigantic task to invent a set of symbols for different modes of expression of all these elements. The best form of symbols for this language must, therefore, consist of picture-notation, painting and sculpture forming its literature. The terminology and the technique of the language is perfected in the *Natyasastra* of the Hindus, and rhythm is indicated by the syllables Ta, Dhi, To, Na, etc. But the artificial side of the language has been developed to a great extent. The railway signals, the military and naval signals, with colour distinctions of green and red, are all of the artificial kind. Military drill and organised games, whether for the young or the old, form a branch also of the language. For all these forms a notation is very necessary.

Of the three forms of language, the notation for music seems to be the easiest. It has only thirteen sounds to represent. Time is also very easy to record; only an intelligent analysis of the structure of the language is required. Western musicians have perfected their notation for music, there being two kinds of it—the staff notation and tonic-solfa. The latter resembles the Hindu system, though not so convenient.

It is now wrongly supposed by some, as by ourselves a dozen years ago, that the method of recording Indian music by means of the letters Sa, Ri, Ga, Ma, etc. is very crude, and that the staff notation of the West should be substituted. This opinion involves a psychological blunder. Early Indian music writers have so cleverly selected the names of the notes that they are capable of being committed to memory easily and sung with the greatest rapidity. Musical instruction begins with singing the notes Sa, Ri, Ga, Ma, etc. By constant practice a reflex action is established in the brain, by which the mere remembrance of the letter Sa or Ri takes the voice at once to its proper pitch, and an Indian singer displays, therefore, a wonderful capacity for singing songs by means of the names of the notes only (and not by the dumb syllables La, la, la, as done in the West), and also extemporises a varied combination of notes so as to produce the greatest artistic effect.

Let us see what psychic processes take place when we see a note Sa, Ri or Ga written on paper. The image of the letter is conveyed to the brain through the optic nerve ; by simple association its name is ascertained, and the impression is transferred to the nerve controlling the vocal chords, and then the correct pitch of the note is sung. The actions that are involved in this case are (1) formation of the visual image, (2) association of image and its name, (3) reflex action between name and pitch. Let us see the mental processes involved in the use of the staff notation: (1) the image of the note is conveyed to the brain, (2) an enquiry is set up as to the name of the note with reference to the clef and the key signature, (3) association of the name, (4) reflex action of the remembrance of the name of the note and its pitch. It will be seen that in the use of the staff notation an extra psychic feat in the second stage is involved. The same symbol also represents seven different notes. The crotchet is the chameleon on the hedge. It changes its colour, its form and its name. The staff notation is, therefore, seven times as difficult as the Indian notation. The wide space it occupies and the special writing materials it requires make its adoption very difficult. The native notation is a picture for the ear, while the staff notation is for the eye: and it is, therefore, very necessary to improve the existing symbols so that they may accurately represent pitch, time and grace, and leave the staff notation to the music of the West.

CHAPTER VIII.

The Ragas

A RAGA is a melodious combination of musical notes which succeed one another. Its effect depends upon the nature of the notes combined. It is like a mixture the quality of which depends upon the nature of its ingredients. It has been pointed out before that every note in the octave conveys a definite feeling—S, P, are agreeable; R_1, G_1 are disagreeable; R_2, G_2, M_1 are free from disagreeableness; and M_2 is painful—and a combination of such notes, which form a raga therefore expresses a definite emotion.

In Indian literature, emotions are divided into nine classes:—

> Sringara Hasya Karuna Roudra Vira Bhayaṇakah
> Bhibhatsa adbhuta santascha Rasah purvai rudahritah

corresponding to love, ludicrousness, tenderness, anger, heroism, fear, disgust, wonder and peacefulness. In Western works on mental science the number of emotions or passions is still greater. From an analysis of musical notes, as made in the foregoing chapter, it is clearly seen that music can give expression only to one kind of feeling, *i.e.*, tenderness, growing from an agreeable state to the disagreeable, and thence to pain by gradual degrees. This is the real nature of simple musical notes, and Shakepeare is right when he says, " I am never merry when I hear sweet music"; for in the octave there are more plaintive notes than mirthful ones. But it is also a matter of experience that music can give rise to the emotions of heroism, terror, sorrow or anger. How is this possible? These varieties of emotion are expressed in music by the proper use of the adjuncts of musical notes, namely, time, pitch and grace, in addition to colour. For example, the voice or tone of anger rises by long intervals. If a raga is to express this emotion, it must contain notes which are at long intervals and be capable of being sung in a quick movement. The nervous system of a person in this mood is in an excited condition and is full of energy. The out-burst of emotion exhibits itself in notes of long intervals. In the case of a person afflicted with pain or sorrow all his spirits are drooping; he speaks in a connected and dragging way. His voice has no strength to take long jumps. In the case of ragas which express pain, sorrow, or disappointment, the notes must never be at a great distance from each other. The help of the graces or Gamakas is very important. We will take only the Kampitam, Humpitam, Linum, and Andolitam, and show how and when they are to be used for the sake of emotion. Kampitam is tremor. The voice trembles only when agitated under certain feelings, such as fear, terror and pain. When a note is accompanied with Kampitam it expresses strong excitement. Sita was alone in the Parnasala when Rama went out in pursuit of the golden deer; and when the giant, Ravana, stood before her in all his hideousness her voice must have been influenced by Kampitam. Humpitam is a grace which indicates strength, courage and heroism. As its name indicates, it is emitted thus, *hum hum*. A lion's roar begins with humpitam; a deadly cannon ball leaves the muzzle with humpitam; the arrow leaves the bow with humpitam; when two fast-going trains cross each other, they produce humpitam. The dholi bearers sing songs full of humpitam, and humpitam added to a note gives strength and force to its expression. Andolitam is swinging; a baby begins its cry by a series of andolitams. Andolitam gives rise to mirth. The voice of bashfulness and coquetry is full of andolitam. Linum is a tender grace, the merging of one note slowly into another. It is used to show relief from pain or anxiety. Linums from M to P and N to S are very beautiful. A sick person finds comfort in groaning, in which Linum is used. The staccato has no place recognised in Indian music, though largely used. It denotes terror. The violent lightening ends in a staccato. A man in a strong fit of rage uses many staccatos. In this way the graces are very important factors, which determine the expressive power of feeling in ragas.

Time is also another factor to be considered. The time of a tune in which there is no excitement must correspond to that of the beating of the heart in the human body. For, as described before, it is the heart that has trained the nervous system from infancy in rhythmic principles. Since its beats increase under excitement, the time of music in such moods must be quick. Hence martial music is always of a quick movement, as in *The March of the Highlanders.* In grief the movement must be slow. The heart is failing. The circulation of blood is slower. Music in such a condition must be of a slow movement, as in *The Funeral March.*

Plato has said that the high Lydian is plaintive, the Ionian and Lydian are soft and convival. The Dorian is the music of courage and the Phrygian of temperance. Aristotle agrees in general, but considers the Phrygian music as exciting and orgiastic, or highly passionate. We fear that both Plato and Aristotle had no proper data on which to base their conclusions. Music cannot express courage or excitement without the help of time, timbre and grace, as shown above, and the feelings of these modes could be analysed clearly and proved as incapable of expressing the emotions ascribed to them. Proceeding in this way, it is not very difficult to construct ragas or compose songs to express particular states of feelings and emotions. Since every mental state has its own characteristic physical expression, every picture could be expressed by means of a raga, and conversely every raga could be analysed and its emotion defined, and also embodied, by means of a pictorial representation. In some sankrit works, several ragas are represented by means of pictures. For instance, *Bhyran* raga is represented by Siva. *Sindhee* is represented by a female figure, who is clothed in red garments. *Gouree.*—This young brunette has adopted the blossom of the mango for her ornament. She is endeavouring to sing her favourite melody, but is too infatuated and intoxicated to proceed with it. *Lulit.*—It is not satisfactorily explained why this beautifully fair creature, who is so overpowered with grief by the absence of her lover, should decorate herself with all her finery of dress, jewellery and flowers. *Depuk.*—The flame which the ancient musicians are said to have kindled by the performance of this raga is depicted in his fiery countenance and red vestments. A string of large pearls is thrown round his neck, and he is mounted on a furious elephant and

accompanied by several women. These representations are only fanciful, and have no connection with the emotions they give rise to, nor do they stand the test of psychology, as discussed above.

We may now be permitted to select a few ragas and explain their emotions. Take Sankarabharana, or the Bilaval of the Hindustani system. It takes Sa, Ri_2, Ga_2, Ma_1, Pa, Dha_2, Ni_2, S. In the lower plane of consciousness melancholy notes Ri_1, Ga_1, Ma_2, are absent. In the higher, the only note of slightly uneasy but thoughtful nature is Ni_2. There is perception, inquiry and dignity in the raga. On the whole, the emotion of the raga is of a calm, and majestic nature. Change Ma into Ma_2. Instead of dignity and courage we feel self-effacement. The main difference between ragas containing Suddha and Tivra Ma is that the former ragas express a feeling in which there is self-reliance, while the latter ones are of a weak self, full of cowardice. Again the Mohana, or Bhup, takes Sa, Ri_2, Ga_2, Pa, Dha_2, Sa. There is no pain in this raga ; for Ri_1, Ga_1, Ma_2, Ni_2, are missing. The notes are at long intervals. It is, therefore, a raga that expresses excitement without any sorrow or pain. The Varali,—this raga takes Sa, Ri_1, Ga_1, Ma_2, Pa, Dha and Ni_2. Except Pa and Dha all the rest are most unhappy. It is termed Soka (pain) Varali, because its emotion is sorrow. The great Tyagaraja has sung the virtues of sage Narada, in this raga thus: "Varanarada." Why? Fearing that direct prayers, addressed to Sri Rama by himself, might not be productive of good, Tyagaraja placed himself at the feet of Narada, surrendered himself, and sang this beautiful composition, praying that he might be lifted up from the miserable condition. Without multiplying examples from the wonderful compositions of Tyagaraja, we will make a short reference to the *Vakra ragas*, in which the ascent and descent of notes is crooked. Here the emotion depends upon the notes selected, but in the course of their development great circumspection, forethought and caution are exercised. The mind thinks twice before it does, and great interest is sustained by the serpentine movements of emotion.

We shall now illustrate, by reference to a picture, the meaning of the musical notes and the ragas. Viswamitra, in the figure before us, was a great rishi (saint) of extraordinary intellectual and spiritual powers. By force of his penance he could command the elements of nature, and once he created a heaven (Swarga) of his own in defiance of the power of the Devas. While he was absorbed in deep meditation in his hermitage, the angels grew jealous of him, and in order to obstruct his meditation they engaged the heavenly nymph, Menaka, to entice him away from his meditation into the enjoyment of carnal pleasures. Accordingly, she started on her mission to the hermitage of the Rishi and captivated his heart by the charms of her beauty. Poor Viswamitra! He yielded to temptation, and the offspring of their love was the baby, Sakuntala. Some months after the birth of the child, Menaka carried it to the hermitage and presented it to its father. Was Viswamitra its father? What a shame for a rishi to acknowledge the fact! Stricken with conscience he hides his face.

Judging from a musical point of view, we find that the baby Sakuntala is fresh born, and is unswayed by every emotion. The baby must be in a condition of deep sleep to represent the shadja, or the first note of the octave. No raga suits its voice. It cries within a range of three or four notes (S, R, G, M), but these four notes only do not constitute any raga. In being lifted up in the air rather in an uncomfortable manner, the intelligent baby has opened its eyes wide and exhibits the note R_2.

The facial expression of Menaka is very attractive. It is not tranquillity, so it is not S. It is not mere disturbance or perception, so it is not R_1 or R_2. It does not mean uneasiness, for she is in a more advanced state of emotion than in G_1 But she is in the mood of enquiry, or ascertaining from the rishi whether he will accept the baby as his or not. Her countenance does not represent M, for there is no egoism in her as when she enticed him, but she is now his subordinate. M_2 is not the expression, for she is not despondent. Hence her face represents G_2. If Viswamitra had acknowledged the child as his own, and if he had been pleased, as a father, with his child, his countenance would have been merry and indicated P, and the three faces would have represented the major

Menaka and Visvamitra,
G2. M2.

chord SGP; but now the child is staring, Menaka is enquiring, and Viswamitra humbled; the three faces indicate R_2; G_2, M_2, which is as discordant to the ear as the picture is to the eye.

Let us see what raga would suit the couple if each was to give vent to the feelings through music, without any words accompanying. Menaka is not certainly in a sorrowful mood. She is conscious of her former triumph. She is only respectful and enquiring. R_1, G_1, M_2 are not appropriate. So the notes must be S, R_2, G_2, M_1, P, D_2, N_2 S which gives us Shankarabharana or Bilaval. She is not in an excited condition as he is. Her raga contains all the seven notes, and the movements must be calm and dignified with many *andolitams.* The *Raga alapa*, or music, would mean like what follows, if it could be translated into the word-language. Menaka holds the baby in her hand, and addresses Visvamitra.

NOTES:—S a a a a a a a a a a a (tranquillity)
I am Menaka.
G R S a a a a a a a a a a a
I am your Menaka.
M G R S a a a a a a a a a a
I am your beloved Menaka.
M G M P D N S a a a a a a a a a a (Perception
Look at me; surely, I am your love.
S N D P M G R S a a a a a a a a
I, your love, have come to you again.
R i i i i i i i i
This is your baby, is it not?
P M G M G R i i i i i i i
Do you see how beautiful it is?
G M D P M G R i i i i i i i
How nice are its limbs?
G a a a a a a a a a a a a (enquiry)
Imagine how matters stand now.
G M P D P M G a a a a a a a a a a
Is it proper that you should thus neglect us?
M a a a a a a a a a a (Egoism)
I am the heavenly nymph.
G M P D P M a a a a a a a
I live with angels divine.

S N D P M a a a a a a a a a a

Believe me, I am angelic in my form.

The above music and its meaning represent the barest skeleton of raga-alapana, which may be continued for hours together. The meaning given above of the music is not actually as represented here, but similar in expressing pathos, entreaties, appeals, threats and persuasions. When, with the help of the graces, skilful variations are introduced, the singing of Menaka becomes more eloquent and forcible than the oration of the greatest orator in the world.

Let us consider the position of Viswamitra. Before she appeared with the child, he was peaceful as at S. When he looked at her, there was perception at R_2, there was uneasiness at G_1, and sudden pain due to the prick of conscience, which took the voice to M_2 and then P and higher corresponding notes. This would give us the Kalyani raga The P is to be rarely used. There is no use of Graha and Nyasa Swaras. The movement of the notes must be quick, as he is excited. Kampitam, humpitam and staccatos are freely used. Such is the raga which the Rishi would naturally use for his mental state.

But if the character of Menaka had differed from that depicted above, and she had been a timid creature like Sakuntala, the raga would have been quite different. R_1 and G_1 would have been used, giving raga Todi with kampitam and andolitam. Every raga thus represents an emotion suited to a particular state of mind.

It is very interesting to note, that several beautiful impressions, created on the mind by ocular phenomena, are transferred, by association of ideas, to the auditory field, and gives rise to very agreeable sensations. An arrow or a meteor shoots through the air, and when a musical sound imitates its motion, and proceeds with rapidity from one note to another, it gives rise to a beautiful feeling. Geometrical curves of different shapes please the mind, and so do the musical notes which constitute curves of different forms, or which rise and fall in progression.

S a a a represents a straight line ————————

SR, SR, SR ◡⌒◡⌒◡⌒◡⌒◡⌒

A slur represents ⌒⌒⌒⌒⌒⌒⌒⌒⌒⌒

A tremor ~~~~~~~~~~~~~~~~~~~~

Staccatos — — — — — —

S, S R, S R G, S R G M

P, M P D, G M P D N,

S R G M, R G M P, &c.

In this way the flow of emotion traces beautiful geometrical figures, and the charms of music are greatly enhanced by a knowledge of such forms of movement.

We have all watched, while we were boys at least, the beautiful motion of kites in the air. In the gust of wind they rise suddenly, flutter for awhile, and fall to the ground—

S R G M P D S a a a a S N D P M G R S

A vulture soars to the sky, hangs quite motionless for a time in search for its prey, and pounces upon it—

S R G M P D N S a S

A tame dove goes up into the sky, in ever-widening circles, and descends similarly with one or two somersaults in each circle—

S R G R S, R G M G R, G M P M G, M P D P M, and back. This represents a simple circular motion.

S R G a M G R S, R G M a P M G R, G M P a D P M G, represents single somersaults. The greater the range of the notes, the wider will be the circle.

S R G a M G R i G R S, R G M a P M Ga M G R, represents double somersaults.

All these examples may be sung calmly, and their accuracy tested by means of vocal music. Every beautiful motion that we see with our eyes has its counterpart produced in the mind through the sound waves, and also expressed by means of figures and gestures. Vocal musicians are in the habit of moving their hands in various ways only to represent the nature of the motion of the sound. In cases of exaggeration, some move their hands as if they are grinding corn; others as if they are pounding rice, while not a small number shake their limbs as if they are seized with convulsive fits. A clever musician, so goes the tradition, once went on a professional tour, and during his varied travels he had to halt for a night in a small village, where the rustics had never tasted the sweets of the art of music. A number of them collected round the musician, who began his performance by singing a few beautiful songs. Nothing attracted the simple folk so much as the trembling of his hand and the shaking of his head. Their attention became more and more concentrated, and the musician spared no pains to display to them his best talent. Having never seen a physical feat of this kind, the audience came to the conclusion that the performer was really seized with a severe convulsive fit, as their cattle and sheep are sometimes wont to have, and, devising a very simple but very effective means of cure, they procured two red-hot irons, branded him in a few prominent parts of the body, and thus restored him to his equilibrium. We are not told, however, whether the musician continued his tours from that time.

This story, though we must pity the poor musician, illustrates in an exaggerated form the principle which we mentioned in the beginning, that every mental state has its corresponding physical expression. "There are two parallel series of changes, one physical (brain-disturbance), one psychical (mental process), occurring together but differing essentially in nature so far as our present knowledge goes. This view of connection between the mind and the body is known as the theory of psyco-physical parallelism" (Brackenbury). Music is an emotional language, and emotion has, of course, its modes of exhibiting itself physically. While it is tracing curves of different forms on the field of imagination the musician moves his hands and facial muscles quite automatically, as a result of the reflex action, in forms corresponding to his mental states. Here is exemplified the co-operation of the three forms of language—the sound-language, the sign-language and the word-language. It is, therefore, unnatural to expect a musician to sit statue-like with folded arms, and give forth his best music. Why should the orator or the actor not repeat his part like a sermon and then retire? The art of elocution and dramatic representation will be a farce without the use of the sign language. Musicians are, therefore, quite justified in using appropriate signs, and he who sings with a cold face at 85° detracts much from the effect of the art.

CHAPTER IX.

Melody and Harmony

IT has long been a subject of the greatest controversy among scholars as to which of the two systems of music—the Eastern or the Western—is superior. It is a very old statement that Indian music is based upon melody and European music on harmony ; melody being defined as a succession of single sounds, and harmony as a simultaneous production of different sounds. Rousseau is of opinion that music is not really improved by harmony. Dr. Burney is doubtful as to which is better. Tartini asserts that music is the offspring of harmony. It is very surprising also that Sir S. Mohan Tagore, of Calcutta, has discovered that harmony is a refinement on melody. Still nobody has clearly explained the difference between the two systems.

For the purposes of this paper we divide all emotions into two classes—internal or noumenal, and external or phenomenal. Emotions, such as love, hatred, anger, pity, are emotions which spring from the heart, and are, therefore, called internal emotions; but those of terror, wonder, that get into the heart from the influence of external objects of nature, are external emotions. It is the melody of Indian music alone that can express internal emotions faithfully, and it is the harmony of the West that can express the external emotion. Melody primarily succeeds emotion, while harmony preceeds it. The function of melody is quite different from that of harmony, and one does not overlap the other. Harmony infuses emotion into the heart, while melody expresses it. Harmony lets emotion in, and melody lets it out. Melody unites or repels two hearts, while harmony unites them with nature. Melody requires, therefore, generally one voice, and harmony more than one. It is this primary distinction that separates entirely one system from the other.

But the objection to the melodies of Western music is' that harmony is introduced in songs which express the emotion proceeding from the heart The side note to the melody called the concord is only a discord, a disturbance detracting from the general effect. What is the purpose of harmony in such songs as "*Goodbye, Sweetheart, Goodbye.*" When the soldier is bidding goodbye to his sweetheart with a single voice, are not other sounds, accompanying, a source of disturbance?

When two lovers are engaged in amorous conversation, or when a devout bhakta is in communion with God, any other sound, however sweet it may be at other times, is a painful disturbance. While Menaka was conversing with Viswamitra, the baby could not be expected to be quiet. It may cry in a range of three or four notes. If these notes are made to blend musically with those of Menaka, they do form agreeable and natural concords, which tend to heighten the emotion of the situation. Beyond the notes of the cry of the baby it is against nature to add any other concords to the singing of Menaka.

When a feeling agitates a person, it exhibits itself by means of a continued voice, which is only a flow of a single sound varying in pitch here and there. On analysis it will be found to resemble a chain of single notes, which succeed one another. It is impossible that at the same time two notes can sound together, and in melody which expresses the feeling of the heart single sounds succeed one another. In Indian music, which is melodic in character, only a single person sings, and the accompaniments, either vocal or instrumental, assist in emphasing the effect of single sounds.

When a person stands on the shores of a mighty ocean, a feeling of grandeur enters into the heart. The waves beat against the shore in rapid succession, various birds hover over it here and there, with their sweet sounds. The hissing of the wind and the bustle of the people add a charm to the scene. What kind of music can express the feeling there aroused? It is only the harmony of the west. One instrument expresses the splashing of the wave; another represents the hissing of the wind; a third represents the cries of the birds; and a fourth expresses the sounds of human voices. All these sounds, though each varies in intensity in its own course, proceed simultaneously, and constitute music, which is termed harmony in the West.

Indian music expresses the pleasures and sorrows of love, the ravings of a mad man, the devout feelings of a bhakta towards God, the tender love of a mother to her child. It can well express all personal feelings which the heart is capable of giving expression to. Isolated sounds of thunder, or the singing of birds, can be expressed in Indian music, but it cannot produce the general effect of grandeur which a simultaneous production of different sounds through different instruments is capable of giving rise to.

Harmony might be introduced in the beginning of our story when Menaka enters the hermitage of the Rishi, while he is absorbed in penance. The cooing of the birds of the forest, the jingling of her ornaments, and the tramp of her feet by the side of a murmuring brook, would afford sufficient material for the use of harmony, which should at once change into melody as soon as the conversation begins.

We may add that the practice of singing songs together by different persons, as soprano, alto, tenor, bass, etc., has no counterpart in nature, and cannot reasonably add to the beauty of the song and increase its emotion. For example

G Ra. R Ma. G P G D a a a Sa S D M Ri M-*Soprano*
Through clustered bloom of April trees, murmurs the evening.

N Ni D Sa Da Ni Da Sa Ma M S D Da W N- *Alto*
Through clustered bloom of April trees, murmurs the evening.

P Pa D Da Ma G P. Sa M Da D M S Ni R.- *Tenor*
Through clustered bloom of April trees, murmurs the evening.

G G M Riii Pa Pa Ma G Ri Ma R *Bass*
Through clustered bloom of April trees . . . .

In the above passage a number of voices are used at one and the same time, and each voice produces a different note. So many different impressions are thrust upon the mind that it is unable to concentrate the attention upon any one of them and appreciate its beauty. The feeling of pleasure aroused is a massive one. Can we get examples from our daily experience of harmony in the sense as understood in the West, *i.e.*, of the same emotion expressed by a number of voices of different pitch simultaneously? When a ship is sinking, when a house is on fire, or when a large number of persons are engaged in a quarrel, or when a number of persons shout, or where a big fight is going on, we have instances of several voices expressing the same emotion; but here we have only sudden and short-lived outbursts of emotion, uttered in the height of excitement, which do not constitute proper material for use in harmony The element of harmony of the West is present in nature more where there is discord rather than concord. Absence of proper illustrations from nature, of the existence of harmony for the expression of internal emotion strengthens our view that it is only a work of artificial innovation.

It is worth while to point out that the element of harmony in the chord is a collective sound, to which no emotional value can be attached. For example, S denotes tranquillity, G enquiry and P mirth. S, G, P, according to Western notion, is a major chord and it leaves upon the mind only a feeling of completeness of pleasure, all the separate emotions of the notes being made up into one. A series of chords which constitutes harmony is thus a chain of agreeable or disagreeable compound sounds, which have lost their individual emotional value by admixture, and which cannot give rise to any sustained specific emotion, since they have no parallel in human experience. Where, as in India, the same melody is played or sung in unison on a number of instruments, such as the veena, the violin, the harmonium and jalatarang, or by several voices, the music produced does not constitute "harmony," as understood in the West. It is the real harmony of nature, in which the emotion of one note is intensified by the co-operation of the same note from a different instrument, but not smothered by the use of the so-called concord, which is really its discord. In such harmony care ought to be taken that due regard is paid to the elements of the sublime and the beautiful, as will be explained in the next chapter. Examples of such united emotion, though rare, could be found when a number of soldiers is proceeding to the front for fighting, or when a festive assembly is engaged in the celebration of a public function. The selection of songs for combined singing should be made with due care as to its suitability for such a purpose.

True, Pythagoras refers to the music of the spheres, sometimes called the harmony of the spheres. We question the truth of his statement. It was not based upon practical observation; for no mortal ear can hear the harmony, and Pythagoras does not claim any supernatural wisdom. He surmises that since the heavenly bodies revolve with a high rate of velocity, and in an order they must give rise to musical sounds that constitute harmony. The earth on which we live belongs to the system of the spheres. If it gives out any note, as every other planet is supposed to do, we should be able to hear it, just as well as Pythagoras. The mermaid's song and the music of the spheres are all in the domain of romance, and have no scientific value. Sir Isaac Newton and Kepler have deduced important laws of gravity, and they have not heard of the celestial music. Now that the mass, velocity, and revolution of the planets are known, we leave it to the scientist to investigate, for the benefit of the layman, if the vibrations of the planets are strong enough to give rise to any sounds at all, as suggested by Pythagoras.

It may be questioned as to how it is that harmony is appreciated so widely by different nations in Europe and America, and that it is making its way into India also. The answer is simple. The human brain is a very fertile mechanism, and when it makes an invention in which a display of skill is involved, it finds many admirers who evince the greatest interest in its acquisition, as well as appreciation. All games which afford pleasure in their exercise are examples of this assertion. If we analyse what charm there is in cricket, chess, cards or the paper-chase we shall find how, even with materials which are by themselves totally void of any higher purpose, artifice can weave a web of imaginative pleasure, and attract a host of admirers. The material of cricket is a ball and a few sticks; of cards, meaningless dots of different colours on paper. When we see how fortunes are staked on the results of cricket matches, and how intoxicated are players while engaged in cards, is there any wonder that harmony should find a large number of supporters, constituted, as its material is, of sweet musical sounds which are singly, or in combination, capable of giving rise to pleasurable sensation?

Melody is music of one dimension, and can trace only linear figures in the field of imagination. Harmony may be of any number of dimensions, and any solid figures can be built out of it. If it is only imaginary "to build castles in the air" to lay persons, it is a reality to the musician. Out of the material of sound, he builds castles and palaces of grand description, lives in them, and feels happy in them; and we may find many such works of art in the famous works of Beethoven and Wagner, who are held as masters of harmony. In architecture, materials of different size and quality are supplied by brick, stone, mortar, wood and metal; but in harmony sounds of various colour or timbre form the material, with variations of time, pitch and grace, supplied by instruments of wind, string and percussion. All the various types of architecture—the Greek, Roman, Gothic or Saracenic—are there, and it only requires a master mind to call them into being. Erect a building of divine description through the help of harmony, and fill it up with spirit by means of melody, and there the mission of the art of music ends.

CHAPTER X.

The Sublime and the Beautiful

THERE are two æsthetic emotions—beauty and sublimity—which form the basis of the study of all the fine arts. Burke, Alison, Payne Knight, Hume, and many ancient Greek philosophers have written at length upon the nature of these emotions, and the part they play in giving rise to pleasurable sensations in the human mind. Alexander Walker says, in his book on *Beauty in Women*, "The characters of beauty or prettiness, with relation to ourselves, are smallness, subordination or subjection. Hence female beauty in relation to the male. The character of grandeur or sublimity, with relation to ourselves, are greatness, superordination or power. Hence male beauty, in relation to female." Payne Knight says:—"All degrees of magnitude contribute to beauty in proportion as they show objects to be perfect in their kind." It may be said that physical littleness contributes to emotion of beauty, and physical superiority to sublimity.

"Nothing is sublime that is not vast or powerful, or does not make one feel sensible of its physical or moral superiority. The simplest cause of sublimity is presented by all objects of vast magnitude or extent—a seemingly boundless plain, the sky, the ocean, etc., with the ideas of height, breadth of resistence, depth of danger, etc., and the simplest cause of beauty being tenderness. As we are concerned in music only with sounds, we have to see which sounds are beautiful and which sublime. Since by association of ideas, a sound reminds us of its physical cause, every sound proceeding from a sublime object is sublime in quality, and a sound produced by a beautiful thing is beautiful, and nature is so skilful in her design of creation that she has blessed a beautiful form with a beautiful voice, and a sublime form with a sublime one. A woman's voice is sweet; that of a man is deep and sublime. The roar is suitable to the lion; the song is appropriate to the cuckoo. Exceptions to this arrangement do exist in nature, but they are ludicrous. A man with a woman's voice, a woman with a manly voice, are unpleasant. Storms, tempests, hurricanes, earthquakes, volcanoes, the roar of the lion, of the elephant, of the bull, etc., excite sublime ideas. The cooing of the dove, the song of the lark or the cuckoo, the voice of a woman, are beautiful.

It must be noted that one and the same object, retaining the proportion of parts, changes its nature from beautiful to sublime, or *vice versa.* An elephant creates sublime feelings, while a horse or a peacock infuses beautiful ideas. Suppose the elephant grows smaller and smaller till it becomes small enough to rest on the palm of one's hand, and suppose the horse grows bigger and bigger till it reaches the skies. What is the change in the condition of the emotions? They have changed places. The horse becomes sublime and the elephant beautiful. As every parent knows, the tender emotion felt towards the baby changes gradually and assumes different forms as it grows from childhood to manhood.

In the same manner, sounds are beautiful or sublime according to their quality, colour or timbre, and it is, therefore, absolutely necessary to use sounds of a particular quality for the expression of particular emotions.

Let us now divide musicial sounds according to their quality. Music is vocal or instrumental. Instruments may be of string, wind or percussion. The veena, the lyre, the piano, the guitar are of the first kind. The harmonium, the flute, the piccolo, the clarionet, the bassoon, the trombone and the trumpet are wind instruments. The drum is an instrument of percussion. The notes of the veena, the violin and the lyre, and of most stringed instruments, are beautiful. Those of the wind instruments are generally sublime. The bass notes are sublime and those of soprano are beautiful. Beauty, being pretty, can appeal only from near; and sublimity, being grand, can best be appreciated from a distance.

It is, therefore, necessary to select suitable instruments to express particular emotions. If a raga is sung by the lion in "Androcles and the Lion," the instrument to be used to voice the feelings of the king of the beasts must be the bassoon or the trumpet, and the notes used s_1 r g m p d n, forming the Todi raga, which is a plaintive melody; but for Androcles a flute, or, much better, a violin will best represent his voice. In the "Lion in love" a trombone would express the feelings of the lion, while a veena or a lyre should be selected for the girl for the expression of feelings. The quality of sound is, therefore, an important factor which determines the sublime or the beautiful nature of the emotion expressed.

If we examine the Western musicians in the light of the two-fold classification of emotions as made above, we shall find that, though they have thoroughly studied the nature and elements of the beautiful and the sublime, they have hopelessly mixed up the emotions in the art of music. In the biggest orchestras, nearly three to four thousand players take part; a hundred or two will be violins, three or four hundred flutes, and as many will be piccolos, and every instrument will thus be represented not by dozens but hundreds, and a thousand voices may be added on to these, as in the Trienniel Handel Festival, celebrated in the Crystal Palace, London, in June, 1912, when the choir and orchestra consisted of 4,000 performers, under the able baton of Sir Frederic Cowen. Tremendous are the powers of discipline and organisation required in a person who has to control such a large body of musicians, but we doubt if what is played is really music. The Westerners are perfect masters in organisation, but can emotion, we mean the musical emotion, spring up under the mechanical command of the rod, in the midst of sounds which are mixed up with no reference to their quality? The blending of the sublime and the beautiful to this alarming extent seems to us entirely unnatural, and for their counterpart in life we have to go only to mechanical organisation brought about by the power of man's supremacy over the creation.

When we get into a thick forest, we find a herd of wild elephants roaming about in large numbers. Far away from them, in another place, we find a number of lions playing in all the liberty of nature. A herd of wild antelopes collect in a third place, and a flight of nice birds of different colours perch here and there in different places. Nowhere in the sphere of creation do we find these animals and birds of different quality living together, and looking upon each other with a feeling of "perfect harmony," except in large circuses, where the ingenuity of man makes the goat and the lion drink and eat in the same pan, or makes the monkey ride upon the elephant. Nowhere in nature do voices of different quality blend harmoniously.

But Indian music is free from blunders of this kind. Even the child knows that vocal music is better than instrumental, and that both are better than dancing. The accompaniments are used only to play a subordinate part to the conductor, who is the chief performer, but not to drown him. The violin or the sarangi is used to help the performer to take his breath, and the drum is used to emphasise the rhythm. The emotion expressed is generally "the beautiful," and all instruments employed are of that quality. The leather used even for the drum is so cured and coated as to change its sound from the sublime to the beautiful, and for use during battles or during busy celebrations, social or religious, wind instruments, called nagaswara, in company with large drums are used. Generally sublime emotions in Indian music are aroused through the help of poetry set to music. The imagination is excited through the words, and not by means of sound. Words do the work of sounds in the Eastern system. The use in the West of all kinds of instruments, even for the expression of tender emotions, is open to strong objection; the same objection applies to the advocates of the harmonium and organ for Indian music. In good music due regard should be paid to the appropriateness of instruments used for the expression of the emotions, the sublime and the beautiful.

CHAPTER XI.

General Observations

WE shall now indulge in a few general remarks on music. We have seen how music acts upon persons of different constitution, and how men susceptible to its influences behave in the world. Music stimulates the nerves of a person very mildly and regulates the flow of blood. It creates a power of concentration in the mind, and spreads an agreeable massive sensation all over the body. The person feels, under the influence of music, disposed to receive impressions from outside. It tills his frame and furrows it, and renders it fertile for the reception and growth of ideas. When, for instance, he hears music while playing cricket, he feels that he has to throw himself heart and soul into the play; when he attends to a religious or social ceremony accompanied with music, he feels that the ceremony has begun and that he should be earnest about it. Music makes light things serious, and invests with a sentiment of reality even imaginary objects. It spreads a charm over the mind, a slight form of intoxication, under which objects appear as if surrounded with an atmosphere of imagination and fancy. It also gives rise to emotion, and sustains it for an indefinite length of time.

The way in which music stimulates the mind is peculiar to itself. Some pastimes, as cards or chess, excite the brain and tax its powers to exhaustion. Some games affect particular limbs and bring on muscular disorder, though they contribute to health and vigour within certain limits. The satisfaction of some of the natural desires is agreeable in the beginning, but ends in satiety and even disgust; for an abnormal degree of activity of the nerve and the muscle is then called into play, which necessitates a period of rest soon after. But in music the stimulation is never too great. The brain is not put to a strain. The whole nervous system of the body enters into a state of vibration, which, being uniform throughout, does not differ much from the normal conditions. There is no loss of energy sustained, but only an equal distribution of it brought about. Its influence begins from the nerve, which it sets in order. Music is, therefore, used as a means of curing certain nervous diseases,—lunacy and other similar affections, which will soon disappear if the diagnosis be correct and the dose well administered. A musical treat given to the lunatics in an asylum is a great source of comfort to the afflicted, and contributes to the betterment of their condition. Music can allay pain, for, as we have pointed out elsewhere, pain is due to an inconvenient vibration of the nerve-cells, caused by some external influence, and music can easily set right such a disorder by means of the regularity of its vibrations. Good music, played during a surgical operation, is a better palliative than the administration of chloroform. In health, music creates a mirthful spirit and acts as a good tonic. In sickness, it acts as a medicine, and is even better, especially in nervous ailments. While medicine acts from the outside, music proceeds from within. Medicine may go wrong and produce evil effects, but music does no harm, even if it cannot succeed. Music is, therefore, said to be a healthy and innocent pastime—always pleasing, but never tiresome.

Is it not pitiable that an art of this nature should be confined to a class of degraded persons, and pronounced as unworthy of cultivation in respectable circles of society? Most musicians in India are uneducated, and, as we have observed already, a musical person without a sound general education is a man without principles. In his hands the art is likely to be abused and looked upon with evil associations; when the musical education goes hand in hand with the general education the art will prove a blessing to mankind, and a source of comfort and pleasure to each and every man.

A few remarks may now be added by way of criticism of the opinion held by some antiquarians, that the Indians have borrowed their musical scale, or at least some of its notes, from the Greeks. This statement proceeds only from an ignorance of the nature of Indian music. It has been explained in the foregoing pages that Indian music is the most natural form of the art, and it takes its material directly from our natural experience. He is the best musician who introduces into his art the most truthful manner of laughing, weeping and sighing, and by such means arouses similar feelings in others. If the Indian learnt how to weep from Pythagoras or how to laugh from Socrates, it is true he borrowed his music from the Greek or the Turk. Both are absurdities.

The only foreign influence that has changed the character of Indian music is the Muhammadan invasion of India, which, we believe, was a blessing in disguise. Music was till then on the stilts and it was the Muhammadan influence that changed its course to the natural channel. Had Indian music developed on the rigid rules which governed it originally, its system would have been quite different from what it is now, and Indian music would have been as mechanical as the harmony of Europe.

The other influence which is now being exerted for the worse on Indian music comes from the West. Western instruments and Western methods have been attracting attention, in preference to Indian, of a section of the public whose powers of appreciation of Indian music are yet to develop. The use of the harmonium for advanced music deprives it of all emotional value. The tone of most harmoniums is neither sublime nor beautiful, and it represents an unnatural voice. The introduction of harmony into Indian music is another evil that is increasing on a large scale. But we are sure that Indian music is based on the firm rock of nature, and no foreign influence can make any deep impression on its surface. Indian painting, sculpture and medicine may yield to Western imitation. The Indian may lose faith in his religion, but the fact remains as clear as daylight that he is not moved by Western music, be he rich or poor, and it cannot, therefore, thrive on Indian soil.

Not only do the systems of music of the East and the West differ from each other in their constitution, but the very modulation of the voice in each shows many points of dissimilarity. Sing as you speak must be the rule. It is said that the Indian sings through the nose, while the Western screams in the throat. Who can decide when doctors disagree? Nature. Nasal singing is natural singing, if nasal sounds are natural sounds. In all alphabets we have two kinds of letters,—the musical vowels, a, e, i, o, u, w and y; and the noisy consonants, which play the most important part in word-formation. L, m, n, and r are also musical. Without the nasal sound, there is no beauty or ease in a language, and an ideal language, divested of its nasals, is most discordant. Healthy nasal sounds give tone and beauty to the sound-language as well as to the word-language. The buzzing of the bee is nasal. The ring of the bell is nasal. The note of the string is nasal. The cry of the infant is nasal. The tones of coquetry and of love are nasal. The moan of the sick person is nasal. The nasal sound is the sound of pain, pleasure, mirth and effort. The very reasonating box of the human voice is situated just behind the nose. Can we avoid the nasal sound? Art requires it, and we shall have it.

Two kinds of voices that are prominent in Western music are the bass and the tenor. One is deep and the other accute. In the production of both the voices the muscles round the glottis appear to be so contracted that the voice appears to be squeezed out. Any attempt to separate art from nature must strongly be deprecated.

But, Western instruments and Western music are not so insipid as represented by a few orthodox musicians. The harmonium is a very useful instrument to begin with. Its tempered nature is no disqualification to its use. When a rough idea of the notes and scales is had, it must make room for a better intrument, the violin or the veena. We do not think it reasonable to state that when the voice or the ear gets itself accustomed to tempered notes, in the early course of instruction, it cannot be altered in an advanced stage. As the mind develops, correct notes may easily be detected and produced. There is no instrument of Indian music which is so simple, easy and portable as the harmonium. The tambura and the veena are useless till a knowledge of tuning is acquired. So is the violin. The harmonium is the only instrument which suits the beginner well. It is the best accompaniment for the stage. The music may not be of a refined type, nor is it possible for every person to become a professor. It is enough if it be popular, but the use of the instrument as a drone by experts, or as an accompaniment to their singing, should strongly be deprecated. No organ, piano or harmonium can produce the delicacies of Indian music. They must be used to serve only as a stepping-stone to an advanced study of the art, to be discarded after a certain course, or occasionally used as a light recreation.

The violin is also an instrument of great capacity. Other instruments of the West are constructed upon such excellent scientific principles, and the intrinsic sweetness of their tone is so charming and perfect, that the Indian will do well to improve his instruments on their model. Great advantage is taken of nature, and high skill and power of invention are displayed in the field of music as in other arts and sciences. The violin, the piano and the harmonium are common. The clarionet, the guitar, the lyre, the flute, the mandoline, the banjo, and a hundred other varieties of instruments of different timbre, supply a most complete set of instruments in English music. The musical boxes, the gramophone, and such like automatic musical machines, form a novelty in Western music. Empty bottles are sometimes converted into a musical instrument; Naked rods of metal and pieces of glass are patched up together to produce music. In some cases, mere bells of different pitch, as in the carillon, constitute a musical instrument. Where have we got such a variety of instruments in Indian music?

The music of the West is also based upon a wonderful system, and its power of imitating the voice of nature is marvellous. It possesses an inexhaustible store of literature contributed by eminent composers of different nationalities, and preserved by means of a well-defined system of notation. The songs are of various kinds, touching upon different topics. Songs on love, devotion, heroism, on friendship; songs on every natural phenomena—the sunrise, the twilight or the gay morning; on every beautiful object—the rose, the butterfly, the will o' the wisp; songs on historical events—the "Death of Nelson" or the "March of the Cameron Men," and songs of all conceivable types, supply the Western musician, be he an amateur or a professional, with a stock which is more than enough for his lifetime, useful to him in his moments of mirth, playfulness, solemnity, pain and pleasure. But light music, simple instruments and a vast literature are, a very great desideratum in Indian music.

The status of a musician in the West is also well defined. Music is looked upon as an accomplishment, and the musician is held in great esteem as one who contributes to social enjoyment and improvement. On his part, he well merits the regard shown to him. He is generally a cultured man and holds a certificate or a degree such as the L.R.A.M., Music Bachelor or Music Doctor. Some musicians are mere coaches, some composers and some performers; each is a specialist in his own line, but contributes to the improvement of the common cause. In India a musician is a failure if he is not a good performer. As there are no examinations in music, even a novice pretends to be equal, if not superior, to an expert, and his superciliousness is encouraged by an innocent audience and an ignorant patron. There is no demand on a large scale for teachers and composers, and men of this stamp, however proficient they may be in their own sphere, are an undesirable set of people in society. When instruction is begun from the sound-language, and when the authorities in India responsible for the education of the country recognise, as in the West, the importance of music in the training of the child as well as the man, the art will attain a position not inferior to any other and musicians, versed either in theory, composition or performance of the art, will all be of service in the great work of the spread of education throughout the length and breadth of the land.

CHAPTER XII.

History of Indian Music.

WE must now turn to the dark side of our picture of music. It is not a pleasant work to point out the mistakes of others, especially of our elders. Though criticism is odious, we cannot dispense with that effective weapon; for, without it there is no road to progress, and it was the critical method that was adopted by most ancient Sanskrit writers on the several branches of learning—logic, grammar or philosophy. They have surveyed all existing works on the subject, criticised them and suggested improvements. This method has given rise to different schools of thought, and has helped the authors to anticipate criticisms from the rival schools and to deal with intricate problems from different points of view. But every writer on music has ignored older works or misunderstood them. Where points were difficult, he has cut a new path of his own, and thus shirked his responsibility. For instance, the *Ratnakara* was written 800 years after the *Natyasastra* of Bharatha. In such an elaborate work as the *Ratnakara*, Sarngadeva did not think it fit to point out the defects of Bharatha, and improve the subject by his own commentaries. Kallinatha, who commentated upon *Ratnakara* 300 years after, has written his work as if *Ratnakara* was a poetic work. Later writers have not followed any of these works.

We must, therefore, in our study of modern music, bear in mind the following words of Miss Margaret Glyn rather than blindly uphold whatever ancient writers have recorded.

> Many of us are no longer satisfied with the methods of our fathers; we percieve the inadequacy of narrow musical judgments founded solely upon technique. We desire to become artists rather than well-informed mechanics; We are seeking in all directions for an intelligible basis of music that will afford foundation for breadth and independence of artistic criticism. Old-fashioned dogmatism will presently be fighting for its life or ceasing to exist. Nature demands survival of the fittest.

Ancient India was truly the land of birth of many arts and sciences, and the fact is undisputed; but when we compare the achievements of the musicians with those of pioneers in other sciences, such as astronomy, medicine, or architecture, we shall find that the musicians have cut a very sorry figure. The astronomer, for instance, had to watch the crooked and imperceptible movements of the heavenly bodies without the aid of any telescope or other delicate instrument. The stars and planets were very elusive and unknown bodies. With all the delay and anxiety in watching their movements, their phases, and their conjunctions, observations have been recorded with the greatest accuracy and have excited the wonder and the admiration of the modern world. The medical man had to go to a forest, pick up an unknown plant, analyse it chemically, discover its properties, try it with risk on human beings under different conditions. Still he has drawn his inferences so accurately that the Hindu medical system stands out even to-day prominent among the medical systems of the world. But the musician whose instruments were only a bamboo and two gourds to serve as a veena (if he was not satisfied with his own chest), or a piece of metallic wire (if his vocal chords did not help him), has not succeeded in his inferences, and has recorded very questionable statements regarding the principles of music. We shall now try to point out a few such blunders, and trace the development of the art more from an artistic point of view than from the scientific.

A few words may be added, in this connection, as to the opinion entertained by some eminent personages that the so-called golden age of Indian music has passed away, and that it began to degenerate centuries ago. An Indian scholar writes:—

"It is clear that its (music) golden age—that period so short in the history of any art cycle and so prepotent in determing the modes of both art and life for long subsequent periods—must be far back from the present. Not improbably, that golden age coincided with the moment of greatest achievement in drama, Kalidasa, and for theory, Bharata. Long anterior to this, however, music was a most highly cultivated of Indian arts—perhaps the most highly cultivated—of Indian arts and to the present day, it has remained that most continuously vital and most universally appreciated art of India."

A student from Calcutta writes to us thus:—

> But it was, and is, really indeed of a perfect theory or practical demonstration of *those Srutis* which the ancients were using, and on the wide and *accurate* application of which they were able to charm nature, make the rain to pour, the fire to blaze, the wind to blow, the stone to melt, &c., &c. That a veena player of the Tanjore Durbar (during the time of Sarabhoji Rao, or so) made the wind to blow, that Muthusawmy Dikshadhar made the rain to pour when he wanted, and that Tansen made the stone to melt, by their music, are not exaggerations. India cannot boast of one single musician who is said to have charmed nature by his music for the last one hundred years or more. This shows that true Indian music began to degenerate, bit by bit, from the beginning of the nineteenth century or earlier, and that the present music of India is much degenerated and corrupted.

It was then great only in quantity but not in quality. Music, as an organism, has developed naturally, and is still developing. It may be safely said that the seeds of Indian music lay scattered wild in nature in pre-historic days. It was sown in the Vedic times. It sprouted in the age of Bharata. Being pruned by the Muhammadan invasion, it bore flowers and yielded fruit in the seventeenth and eighteenth centuries. As a tree of luxuriant growth, it is now surrounded by a few insects, born of the influence of foreign methods, and it is easy to dispel them.

The earliest form of music known to us is the *Sama* chanting. The Sama Veda consists of short pieces called Riks, which require the four notes Pa, Ni, Sa, Ri in their recitation. Here Ni is Ni_2, Ri is Ri_1 ; for, Ni_1, being very plaintive, does not enter into the recitation. Ri_1 is slightly higher than Sa, and very convenient to sing when no further advance is required. After some time the rise and fall of pitch were marked on the inner lines of the fingers of the right hand, as detailed in the *Naradiya Siksha*. The two lines on the thumb were Krista and Pratama. On the first finger there was the note Dvitiya. On the middle finger was Tritiya, Chaturta was on the ring finger, Mandra and Atisvarya stood on the little finger. In its progress from recitation to chanting, R_2 seems to have first crept into ಪ ನ ಸ ರ, P N S R, making it ಪ ನ ಸ ರ ರ, P N S R R_2 . We have not yet come across any scholar who could explain this portion of

Narada Siksha clearly from a scientfic point of view, and show its application to practical purposes with the aid of the flute or other instrument. The feeling of agreeableness resulting from the singing of these sounds was first experienced by our rishis during these chants. They were a class of people very learned in language and literature. They assembled in the forests to perform religious sacrifices, and, when they gradually prolonged the notes for different lengths of time, the element of time entered into the chanting. Also, for relieving the monotony of chanting, the range of all the notes was transposed to a higher pitch. This transposition helped them to the discovery of ಗ ಮ ಧ, G M D and led them to complete the formation of the whole octave, the names of the notes being those as given above. As time rolled on, the ಋತ್ವಿಕ್, Ritwik sought the aid of a number of assistants to relieve him, all of whom joined in the chanting, modulating their voices in various ways to bring the notes into unison. This may be called the Vedic period of music.

While Sama chanting was assuming a definite shape, there was in the process of making, a class of secular persons who attended the sacrifices, and who, carrying home the agreeable impression of the chant of the Riks they had heard in the assemblies, applied themselves to the study of musical notes for purposes other than religious. They began to cultivate the art of singing, and named their notes as Sa, ri, ga, ma, pa, da, and ni, and they reconciled these musical notes with those used in the Sama.

For a time the two classes of singers, religious and secular, proceeded side by side. Afterwards the secular and more ambitious class left their religious brethren far behind, and continued to develop the art of music more scientifically.

To these early music-makers we must be grateful for the selection of the beautiful names Shadja, Rishabha, Gandhara, Madhyama, Panchama, Dhaivata, Nishada. It is difficult to reconcile the derivation of the terms according to their position or tone in the octave. Various interpretations have been given as to the meaning of the word Shadja, one of them is as follows:—

> Nasa Kanta murastalu jihva dantamscha Samsprusan
> Shadbhih Sanjayate Yesmat Tasmat Shadja Udiritah.

This is not satisfactory. It is considered, also, that being a note on the sixth sruti from dha it is named as Shadja. Why of all the notes S alone must be reckoned from dha is neither clear nor satisfactory. Since the other six notes rest upon the fundamental note, it is reasonable to interpret the word Shadja as a note which gives rise to the other six notes. Madhyama and Panchama denote their place in the octave; ri, ga, dha and ni are chosen for the sake of facility in pronouncing the notes during singing. It is a very interesting point to note, that in naming the swaras great attention was paid to obtaining facility in singing. Shadja was contracted into not sha but sa, which is very easy to pronounce. Ra is a letter which even babies delight in crying.—R-r-r-r; Ga is a letter which everyone produces easily; ma is in mamma; pa in papa; the first words that every infant learns in the very beginning; dha ni are soft dental letters. This cleverness of the inventors, due to their high general culture in literature, has supplied Indian music with a melodious series of musical notes in the octave, most easy to sing rapidly. While the ancient musicians were far-seeing in their selection of the names of the notes, they displayed a hopeless want of the grasp of the scientific side of the notes. It is said:—

Shadjam mayuro vadati
Gavas tvrushabha bhashinah
Ajadi kantu Gandharam
Crounchah kvanati Madhyamam
Pushpa sadharanekale
Pikah kujati Panchamam
Dhaivatam heshate vaji
Nishadam brimhate gajah.

The peacock cries *Shadja;* the cow gives out Rishabha; the goat's bleating is of the Gandhara pitch; the *crouncha* bird sings Madhyama; the cuckoo gives out Panchama note; the horse's neighing is Dhaivata; and Nishada is sounded by the elephant.

Many writers pass over these lines with the remark that they show that our ancient writers had some conception of absolute pitch of musical notes. We cannot think so. The object of citing examples is to make difficult points clear;

not the whole world can make this collection of animals and birds give out their note when required, so as to enable the musician, especially the beginner, to judge the pitch of musical notes in the octave.

Again, unless all the peacocks of the present day have altered their tone, there is no sense in the sloka. The peacock, though most beautiful to look at, gives out a shrill repulsive shriek, which is an unpleasant combination of the cat's mewing in curvature, and the crow's cawing in disagreeableness. The range of the cry extends over three notes, and so do the voice of the cow, the goat, the horse and the elephant. The *crouncha* is a very rare bird, though the cuckoo is very common. Who has not heard its melodious notes—Co-o-o? They vary in three degrees, and no two birds give the same pitch. The lowing of the cattle is in the *mandara*, and the goat bleats in the *madya*. The sloka is not only useless for all practical purposes, but also erroneous. We wish that it had not been included in musical treatises, and bequeathed to us as a piece of ancient musical wisdom.

But the worst of it comes when we examine the inner or artistic meaning of the notes, as understood by early music writers: it is said,

> Sari vire dbhute raudre dho bhibbatse bhayanake.
> Karyau ganitu karune hasya sringara yor mapau.

Music, as we stated in the beginning, is a language of emotions, and when we attempt to show how the art can express them we shall have to be very careful in defining our premiss. In the sloka quoted above, it is said, Sa expresses valour; Ri, wonder; Ga, tenderness; Ma, ludicrousness; Pa, love; Dha, disgust; and Ni, kindness. The interpretation of all ragas depends upon the sloka, and the whole meaning of music rests on it. If we closely examine the passage we shall find that the value of *Natyasastra*, *Ratnakara*, and other Sanskrit works on music, reduces itself to nothing. For, it is impossible that any musical note can express the ascribed emotion by itself without the help of time and grace, and what a pity it is that *santi* or peace, which is the most predominent emotion that could be felt in music, is left out of consideration. Not only is this sloka opposed to the principles of psychology, as explained in the early part of this paper, it is also opposed to experience and the notion of rasas, or passions, as explained in standard Sanskrit works. It would have been pardonable if such a statement had proceeded from an illiterate musician, but coming as it does from such eminent scholars of Sanskrit as Bharatha and Sarangadeva, whose general culture and command of the language is simply marvellous, and who have discussed the question of rasas as familiar in their own treatises, their claim to consideration as authorities on music rests on no sure footing. Is it possible for a chemist to have wrong notions of the properties of the very elements of oxygen, hydrogen and nitrogen, and then hope to achieve success in his further investigations?

A musician who is ignorant of the properties, physical as well as æsthetic, of the very fundamental note Sa, is incapable of writing upon the subject of music, and his statements are to be taken at a very great discount.

The inaccuracy of the sloka may be exhibited more clearly in another way. In the octave SP, SM, RD, GN are said to be *samvadis* or consonant pairs of sounds. The emotion of one note must therefore agree with that of the other. According to the sloka, S expresses heroism and P love. In Prathapa Rudriya, a standard work on the definition of *rasas* or passions, heroism is defined thus—

ಲೋಕೋತ್ತರೇಷು ಕಾರ್ಯೇಷು ಸ್ಥೇಯಾನ್ ಪ್ರಯತ್ನಃ ಉತ್ಸಾಹಃ||

Heroism results from a spirit of enterprise and Sringara or love

ತಂತ್ರಸಂಭೋಗವಿಷಯ ಇಚ್ಛಾ ವಿಶೇಷೋರತಿಃ

arises from sexual love; S and P never agree since valour and love are unlike emotions. R expresses wonder and D disgust;

ಅಪೂರ್ವಾರ್ಥಸಂದರ್ಶನಾಚ್ಚಿತ್ತವಿಸ್ತಾರೋ ವಿಸ್ಮಯಃ,
ಅರ್ಥಾನಾಂ ದೋಷಸಂದರ್ಶನಾದಿ ಭಿರ್ಗರ್ಹಣಾಜಿಗುಪ್ಸಾ.

Wonder arises when a sight that had not been seen before is seen and disgust arises from the observation of defective points in a thing. That M can express ludicrousness is itself ludicrous. Thus, notes agreeing in sound are contrediictory in meaning which is not correct.

When the feelings attributed to the musical notes are so inaccurate, especially valour to the fundamental S, can we expect the passions ascribed by these writers to the ragas to be correct? Can the structure stand when the foundation is tottering? It is to be regretted that, as a consequence, the emotions attributed to the ragas by Bharata, and all other subsequent writers, carry no significance and they are positively misleading.

If, in the early period, music writers were incapable of knowing the inner beauty of sound, it may be questioned how it was that they were able to discover the 22 srutis in the octave, which are a source of trouble to eminent men even in our days. A key to this answer may be found from a study of the first two chapters of the *Ratnakara*. Ancient musicians began their subject of music in an atmosphere of metaphysics. Jeeva Karma preritam tada, etc. The Soul, or Jeeva ಜೀವ, enters the mother's womb in consequence of karma. It grows there and develops from month to month. It imbibes passions and emotions by and by. Its chemical and physical compositions undergo various changes and ida, pingala, sushumna nadis, or chords, through which life traverses are considered very important. The sound is said to proceed from three places in the body, as Mandra in the breast, the Madhya in the neck, and the Thara in the head. But the most important point to be noted for our purposes is this

ತಸ್ಯದ್ವಾವಿಂಶತಿರ್ಭೇದಾಃ ಶ್ರವಣಾಚ್ಛ್ರುತಯೋಮತಾಃ |
ಹೃದ್ಯೂರ್ಧ್ವನಾಡೀ ಸಂಲಗ್ನಾನಾಡ್ಯೋದ್ವಾವಿಂಶತಿರ್ಮತಾಃ ||

The sound originating in each place becomes divisible into 22 parts, because they proceed from the 22 nadis or chords, which are supposed to exist above the region of the heart. It was this number 22 of the nadis that suggested the probability of the existence of the 22 srutis. It was also this suggestion that led Sharngadeva to build two veenas in which, though he knew that 22 frets, placed near each other in an octave, could have given him 22 srutis, he preferred the inconvenient method of fastening 22 strings to one veena.

Had it not been for this reason, we fear that the number 22 of the srutis would not have seen the light till to-day; for most practical musicians do not know of the existence of these minute divisions of the octave.

We by no means deprecate the study of the minute division of the octave into 22 divisions, nor are we blind to the fact that in highly refined music the 12 ordinary notes do not serve our purposes, and that even more than 22 notes are required. The use of these notes indicates an advanced degree of musical culture, and they are to be made the subject of study in the higher stage of musical training. It is, therefore, a folly to base the method of primary training in music on the recognition of these minor divisions and adopt a complicate notation for their representation.

The theory of 22 srutis is also refuted by several modern scholars of music, and we have strong reasons to believe in the practical demonstration of the existence of 24 srutis and of their application to the modern ragas of the Karnatic system, made by Rao Sahib Abraham Pandithar Avergal of Tanjore, both at the All-India Conference and also at the residence of V. P. Madhava Rao, Esquire, B.A., C.I.E., Dewan Sahib of Baroda and president of the Reception Committee. According to the Rao Sahib, the Karnatic system, the development of which we have attempted to trace, seems to have existed side by side with the Tamilian system, which is said to have existed for the last 10,000 years. The Tamilian system recognises divisions of the octave into 24, 48 and over; but the great antiquity attributed to it requires historical corroboration, since the system of music now in use in Southern India has more in common with the Tamilian than with the intricate principles laid down in Sanskrit works.

From the time of the Sama Veda onwards, it is not difficult to say that music was slowly advancing as a science. The scales were built out of the 22 srutis, and the music practised during this early period must have resembled more or less the chanting of Sama, but more mechanical.

But after the time of Bharata the popularity of music must have increased considerably, and the golden age of Sanskrit literature begun. The *Sama* chanters completely retired into the background, the musicians got the upper hand. They were considered indispensable to royal courts. They began to compose Sanskrit verses on different subjects and set them to music. This period is the middle period in the history of music. The power of music as a pastime and healthy recreation was well recognised. It found free use in dramas and poetry, as in Jayadeva's *Githa Govinda.* It became more and more definite in form; embellishments, or gamakas, conspicuous by their absence in Bharata, received recognition, and their number is given as 15 in *Ratnakara*, though their definitions or uses are not clear; but it must be said that this middle period, while contributing largely to popularise music and increase its literature, left many traces of its influence which proved harmful to the development of the art, and which are at work even now.

1. It created a wrong notion that poetry and music were inseparable parts of the same artistic body. ಸಂಗೀತಮಪಿ ಸಾಹಿತ್ಯಂ ಸರಸ್ವತ್ಯಾಃಸ್ತನದ್ವಯಂ|| ಏಕಮಾಪಾತಮಧುರಂ ಅನ್ಯದಾಲೋಚನಾಮೃತಂ||.

2. It unnecessarily restricted the time and season for the singing of the ragas.

3. It ascribed supernatural powers to certain ragas, such as bringing rain or kindling fire.

From the analysis of languages, given on page 4 it will be seen that in each class there exist two divisions—prose and poetry. The main difference between the two forms is the presence of rhythm in the latter. If the nature of the rhythm was the same in all kinds of language, poetry, music and dancing would have blended completely. Unfortunately, the principles of word-rhythm are quite different from those of music, and their complete fusion is an impossibility. It is fitting a square into a circle. Good music and good poetry can, therefore, "never live together." One is a drag upon the other and each loses its best traits of character. It is word-prose that blends most beautifully with song. Sound-prose (alapana) unites best with word-language the quite natural. Sound-poetry and word-prose, powers prose and word-poetry, also produce a sweet effect in which poetry somewhat loses its form; but though most inconvenient is the blending of poetry and music in which each descends from its high level, each gains an artistic effect in combination. "To music is added," says Miss M. Glyn, "an intellectual interest and to poetry an emotional force." If sign-poetry, *i.e.*, dancing is also added, as in the Indian nautch, the blending of music, poetry and dancing becomes most effective, and captivates the heart. When applied for a good purpose it forms the best way of expressing one's feelings and emotions. The nautch in which the three highest forms of language are blended is an innocent social enjoyment, and weak-minded members of the anti-nautch party only betray their ignorance of art, and place themselves in the outer musical angle, very close to A in the figure B.

In Jayadeva's *Gita Govinda* we have a combination of poetry and music; both are rhythmic and there is no freedom for the free play of either.

Tyagaraja, of South Indian fame, has embodied his ideas in prose in his immortal songs, which are now the life of South Indian music. Variations, or *Sangatis*, are his most effective weapons used for the expression of passions, and he has fully succeeded in his attempt. Since it was necessary to keep the emotion from straying off the rails, a few words are chosen in the music as pegs to hang emotion upon.

Time and Music

When the desire to combine poetry and music was well established, literature multiplied rapidly, and poems were not wanting, being descriptive of every time of the day, the month, the season and the year. Stanzas were set to some raga and sung accordingly. By frequent repetition, the raga and the stanza fused together. If the raga reminded the stanza, which described the day or the season, the season or the day reminded the raga, by the law of the association of ideas. Gradually the time and the raga became inseparable ideas, though the stanza was forgotten, and it was laid down as a rule by sheer prejudice that no raga ought to be sung at times not prescribed for it.

How baneful is prejudice! It is based upon neither instinct nor reason. It divides humanity into various races, sets up colour differences and makes people hate each other. What are religions but codes of prejudice? The Lord Bishop of ——, who now condemns idol-worship would have prostrated himself before the image of Sri Krishna had he been born as a Hindu. The Mahamahopadyaya of Benares would have grown the longest beard and cried *Allah ho Akbar* if his lot had been cast in Arabia. There is but one God and only one religion; but prejudice has torn every reason to pieces. Let it work its havoc in music also as in politics and religion.

There are therefore morning Ragas, midday Ragas, evening Rages, midnight Ragas, summer Ragas and winter Ragas; male Ragas and female Ragas. While the object of every Raga is to express an emotion without reference to time, where is any sense in confining that emotion to any particular part of the day. Raga Todi, for instance, expresses sorrow and pity. Why should it be fixed for the morning as if every human being is swayed by that emotion in that part of the day? This restriction is born of prejudice and sanctified by antiquity, should be removed, though difficult,. as soon as possible.

It is sure to vanish on a minute examination of the construction of the raga, and if a restriction of this kind is required at all, it must be based on physiological facts. A person is in a vigorous state of mind in the morning, having enjoyed complete rest during the night preceding. His nerves are quite able to withstand strong impulses. There is a great freshness in the mind, and a raga with notes of long jumps, expressing the emotion of courage or strength, will be a fitting raga for mornings. As the day advances the nerves are taxed, and they lose their power to readily respond to outward impulses. They can at this stage yield to notes of a consecutive nature. Such considerations must be the basis of classification of ragas according to the time.

Supernatural Powers of Ragas

In the early part of this chapter a letter is recorded in which it is affirmed that the modern musicians have become degenerated because they cannot cause the rain to pour, or the fire to burn, by means of their music. It is a tendency in all persons that whenever the mind is cast into the dark pages of bygone days, an atmosphere of romance suddenly comes into existence, as in the *Arabian Nights*, and the more the details are absent the more does the imagination create a language of metaphors and exaggeration.

The nature of music and its function are very clearly explained in the beginning of this book. It has been found quite possible to analyse a particular raga, examine its notes, and define the emotion it can give rise to. The power of making the stones melt or causing the rain to fall is not perceptible in any of the ragas, and the ascription of supernatural powers is only a myth. In our anxiety to praise a thing we only condemn it through exaggeration. The music of Gopala Naik or Tan Sain might, at its best, have been as sweet as that of Tyagaraja, but Tyagaraja was never a firebrand or belonged to the fire brigade. His music was of incomparable beauty, exquisite sweetness, and wonderful power of appeal. It may be true that Sri Rama presented himself before him more than once, and it is a statement in which there are germs of truth. When once Tyagaraja went to the famous hill of Venkateswara on the Tirpathi hill, it was the time of worship; a curtain hid the view of Venkateswara from Tyagaraja. The worshippers did not remove it for a very long time. Tyagaraja grew impatient, and began to sing in praise of Him. Immediately the curtain split itself into two, and revealed the majestic figure of the idol. We are inclined to believe the story, for the appealing power of the music of Tyagaraja is so strong that it must have created a very strong impression upon the Almighty, who is all-merciful, and thus secured ready response. Tyagaraja's condition at that time is described thus ಪುಲಕಾಂಕಿತ ಶರೀರ.

Overcome with sentiments of devotion or bhakti, his hair stood on its end, tears flew down his cheeks, he thought that he was actually speaking to God. Will such a devotion go unrewarded? Certainly not. God is merciful. He does respond to His bhaktas. But wind and rain are inanimate, and it is in vain to throw such miraculous powers into ragas indiscriminately. The trees and stones yield to axes and hammers, but not to ragas.

The fact that, though we have excellent musicians in our midst, we cannot bring down even a single drop of rain from the sky proves not that music of the present day is degenerate, but that the power of bringing down rain is not existing in music.

The Method of Tuning

In his very learned book, *The Introduction to the Study of Indian Music*, Mr. Clements says that the method of tuning in ancient days was different from what it is now, and this view is supported by Captain Day. We presume that Dhaivat tuning was in vogue from the time of Bharatha to that of Ahobala, which covers the early, middle, and transitional periods in the history of Indian music. If so, it goes to prove that the musicians of those days cared more for obtaining scientific combinations than artistic ones. It is said that dha, ri, and ga formed the drone notes. The force of the drone, or sruti ಶ್ರುತಿ, in music is like the force of gravity, and attracts every other sound towards it. Before its continuous flow, every other note loses its intrinsic effect, and acquires its meaning upon its relation to the drone. According to psychology, founded upon actual experience, when a musical note is first sounded, every other note that succeeds it is affected by the first sound. When Dha, is used as the drone, Sa, a note which is six srutis from Dha, will compel the ear to treat it as Ga, and compel a corresponding change in the effect of all the other notes, by the process of transposition. Though the notes are sung as s r g m pa dha ni ಸ ರಿ ಗ ಮ ಪ ಧ ನಿ, in effect they will be ಗ ಮ ಪ ಧ ನಿ ಸ ರಿ. It is this unstability of equilibrium of emotion experienced in ಧ್ರುವರ್ tuning, that can reasonably account for the prominence given to Graha, Jeeva and Nyasa notes in the method of combining different ragas.

Most probably the advent of the Muhammadans removed the props, removed the ಧ್ರುವರ್ tuning, introduced S P drones and then gave a background to the picture of the raga. From that time the ಅಂಶ and ಗ್ರಹ notes lost their force, and fell into disuse. They have no scientific or practical value now.

The modern period of Indian music commenced when the Muhammadans established themselves firmly on Indian soil, and put the stamp of their rule on all the activities of their subjects, in matters social, religious and intellectual. Music did not escape that influence. The most important change was the restoration of stable equilibrium of emotion, and the freedom of the raga from the shackles of ಗ್ರಹ and ನ್ಯಾಸ notes. Music assumed a more definite and artistic form. Its parts became more smooth and elastic. Great strides in civilisation were taken; migration from one part of India to another was facilitated; the English also entered India; and the whole land of Aryawartha was under one rule. Art and literature flourished, but no political adjustment could bridge the gulf that separated the northern and southern systems of music. So far as music was concerned, each part of the country developed its own system. Being identical in substance, the Hindustani and Karnatic systems of music differed only in form.

Tan Sen and Gopal Naik are the persons who developed the northern system, while the southern was represented by Tyagaraja of immortal musical fame, Muttu Swami Dixit, Shama Shastrigal, and a host of others, in whose hands modern music attained the perfection of its growth. All the ragas were logically classified; the thalas were well applied. Raga alapana became more ingenious and melodious. The improvised feat of singing what is called Pallavi was perfected. On the whole, music of the present day is in a more highly developed state of vigorous manhood than before.

Owing to the want of encouragement the art has not been cultivated on systematic lines. Time is precious in these days of stress and struggle. Only artists of high repute earn a living by music, while men of ordinary calibre retire into the background. Still the national art is running as widely as before, but only on a lower surface. If the importance of the art is recognised in consideration of its capacity to soften a man's feelings, and encouragement given by the introduction of the art in private houses and public institutions, there is every certainty that it will shine as brilliantly as ever it did. But we are not blind to the danger that besets Indian music at present, through a desire to imitate foreign methods and introduce harmony indiscreetly and adopt foreign instruments. If the cultivation of Indian music is encouraged on national lines, all these dangers are sure to disappear. The indiscriminate use of the harmonium should be checked, and the cultivation of vocal music and the veena, sithar and saringi improved. Indian musical instruments require improvement so far as the richness of their tone is concerned. Instruments of sublime tone are necessary. Attempts are also to be made for composing songs, expressing external emotions, and to introduce the principals of harmony based upon nature.

It is a well-known fact that the arts and industries of a nation reflect its inner life, and we cannot conclude this paper without saying that the scale of music we have been

"THE BOW SPRANG BACK, AND RESOLVED 'HOWL O' NIGHTS' INTO THE FIVE ELEMENTS."

using may be taken as an index of the meaning and purpose of life in this transitory world, as held in Hindu philosophy.

Nada Brahma, Gyananandamaya, the pervader of the universe, is composed of knowledge and joy. The soul, which is a spark of that Great Power, is originally divine and pure. Owing to the influence of *maya*, it comes into the world in the pure state of Shadja, and, passing through the various stages of pain and pleasure in the sphere of the lower self, represented by R_1, R_2, G_1, G_2, M_1, feels disgusted with the world in Ma_2, and reaches the intellectual plain, and, by meditation upon Brahma, it reaches the eternal state, from which it proceeded, and merges again into the higher self in S the octave. But one who gives himself up to sensuality, and turns a deaf ear to the intellectual advancement, remains in the state of Prati Madhyama M_2, a state of Naraka, or eternal pain. May the Almighty God, who is the pervader of the universe in the form of sound, infuse into all beings a spirit of love for intellectual pursuits, and lead them to inquiry through the stages of D_1, D_2, N_1 and N_2, and absorb them into the land of bliss, or reunion with Brahma, in the calm, peaceful state of S, the higher octave.